The Ping Project:

How we trained a diabetic alert dog at home

Narrative Poem
Collin and Ping
It all started when I was six
I had high blood sugar
That needed a fix
It also can go low
Without much warning
Like a blizzard of snow
On a cool dark morning
Who could help me with this task
Not Mom or Dad
Or even a doctor with a mask
The person to help me wasn't
A person at all
It was a wonder dog
Who could smell it all
Her name is Ping
She is as happy as can be
Because keeping me safe is her thing
-by Collin
(November 28 2012, 10 years old)

Dedication
I dedicate this book to Collin, who is strong, brave, smart, funny, cute, and an excellent dog trainer, baseball player, brother, son, grandson, student, friend, and is a type 1 diabetic. Thank you for your dedication in training Ping. I believe that you and Ping are going to change the way D.A.D.s are trained.

Family Christmas (2012). Kendra, Cora, Collin, and Dave.

To Collin's family, Kendra, Dave, Cora and Probie (their Labrador):

Thank you for sharing Collin and Ping with me. I salute you for your hard work and dedication to training Ping; you have done a wonderful job! I would also like to thank you for allowing me to share Collin and Ping's story and photos in order to help others that may choose to train a D.A.D. at home.

To Kendra:

A job well done! Training any dog is hard work, but training a D.A.D. while balancing everything else takes a very special person. I hope Ping brings many years of being your back-up, catching Collin's lows and highs, and bringing you tons of fun.

WARNING!

READ THIS PAGE BEFORE YOU DECIDE TO PURCHASE A DOG OR EVEN THINK ABOUT TRAINING A DIABETIC ALERT DOG!

This book was written to assist in the training of a diabetic alert dog (D.A.D.) at home and is a detailed description of how we trained Ping, a three-month-old rescue dog. Results will vary depending on the dog's intelligence, dedication of the trainer, and consistency of training. No dog learns the same way; so finding someone with dog training knowledge will be helpful when your dog responds differently than expected.

YOU ARE STRONGLY CAUTIONED NOT TO RELY ON ANY DIABETIC ALERT DOG TO THE POINT OF NOT ADHERING TO ALL OTHER MEDICAL PROTOCOLS, TESTING, AND ALL OTHER PROCEDURES THAT WOULD OTHERWISE BE APPROPRIATE IF THERE WERE NO DIABETIC ALERT DOG. NEVER IGNORE OR REDUCE ANY OTHER ADVICE AND INSTRUCTION OF YOUR DOCTOR.

THE AUTHOR AND PUBLISHER OF THIS BOOK MAKE ABSOLUTELY NO WARRANTIES, EXPRESS OR IMPLIED, ABOUT THE INFORMATION AND MATERIALS APPEARING IN THIS BOOK.

USE OF THIS BOOK AND ALL SOURCES WHERE THIS WORK IS QUOTED OR REFERENCED IS ENTIRELY AT THE RISK AND DISCRETION OF THE READER AND OR USER.

The Ping Project- Table of Contents

Foreword

Kendra and Collin

I will admit that I was very uneducated about diabetes prior to November 5, 2008. What I did know, I learned from those commercials with the oatmeal guy. We do not have any history of diabetes in our family, so it was never on my radar. However, I knew something was wrong with my little boy; he just wasn't himself. He was difficult to wake up in the morning, hated going to first grade, napped after school, used the bathroom all the time, and was constantly eating. I didn't know it back then, but he displayed all the classic symptoms.

A few weeks prior to Collin acting this way, my daughter had a bladder infection. Light bulb moment! Collin must have a bladder infection. My husband rushed to drop off a urine sample at the doctor's office. About 11:00 in the morning I received a call from the doctor's office requesting to see Collin. I was told not to feed him lunch, give him anything to drink, and to be safe but get there as quickly as possible. I hurried to pick him up from school and headed to the doctor. It was there that our wonderful doctor told me, with a tear in her eye, that Collin had diabetes. I clearly remember thinking, "That stinks- I guess no more cupcakes for him." She sent us directly to a local hospital where we stayed for three days. I slowly understood why she had tears in her eyes: this was no oatmeal commercial. We learned about giving our six year old five shots daily, carbohydrates, different types of insulin, fast-acting carbs, signs of hypoglycemia, signs of hyperglycemia, and the very real dangers of this disease. The most heartbreaking moment of my life occurred when my sweet blonde-haired blue-eyed boy asked me how long he had to take insulin and how long he would have diabetes. I could feel my heart shatter as I told him the rest of his life.

Four years later, we have adjusted to life with type 1 diabetes. It is now status quo, and I can draw up insulin at a stoplight, the top of a Ferris wheel, or in a movie theater. I am always reading about the new technology in the diabetes world. I love hearing about all of the advances and great technology, but I always came back to the diabetic service dogs. We have always been a dog-loving family, and I started researching D.A.D.s (diabetes alert dogs). I found them fascinating, and I knew this was something that could help Collin, but then I saw the price of these dogs! It was just not an option for our family. This was when I started researching self-training. The information was all very vague and hard to come by to the average person. I contacted my "go-to dog girl", Shari. She was interested but warned me it was going to be a lot of work.

She also told me that we needed to pick a puppy very carefully; it would take a very special dog to take on the role of a D.A.D. I knew that I wanted a shelter dog. This is just who we are as a family. I understand that this is not the best option for everybody. This is just what we wanted as a family. It is also very important to say that we approached this with a strong commitment to our future dog. If the puppy picked up on the training and became a D.A.D., that would be awesome; if not, we were happy to have another pet. We never considered not keeping the dog if she did not do well with scent training.

This training has been so much more work than I imagined. It has also been so much more rewarding and enjoyable than I ever imagined! We love Ping, and she is part of our family. Her training has been time consuming, frustrating, and emotional, but it has also been one of the most wonderful experiences of my life. I love training her with Collin and Shari. I love watching her "get it." She alerts us to Collin's blood sugar, but she also provides Collin comfort when this disease becomes overwhelming. She is his best friend and his lifeguard.

-Kendra Chesney (Collin's mother)

Introduction

My name is Shari Finger, and I developed the protocol illustrated in this book to train Ping as a diabetic alert dog. Since the beginning of this project, I have learned so much about this disease: how it doesn't play fair; takes care-free days from children; and can steal those children from their parents without word nor warning. Where other diseases can go into remission, have symptoms treated with medication, be covered up, or can be cured, children with diabetes never get a break from this affliction; they live with it every minute of every day for the rest of their lives. When I was approached by Kendra, I admit I knew nothing about diabetes, but I did know about dogs.

In the 1980's, I read a story about a search and rescue (SAR) dog. I was intrigued by the ability of a dog being able to smell and locate people under the rubble of a building flattened during an earthquake. I decided I wanted to join a search and rescue team and train a dog of my own. I started by finding everything I could read on search and rescue dogs. I felt it was my calling in life and that someday I was going to save someone's life. In the 80's and 90's, search dogs weren't as common as they are now. You never saw them on TV searching through the aftermath of a disaster, and there weren't any schools or even anyone in my area that I could find that had ever trained a SAR dog.

However, I was obsessed. I am sure a lot of people thought I was a little crazy. After all, I was not a police officer; I owned a national award-winning nail salon and was a nail tech. This all changed on April 19, 1995 when the Alfred P. Mural Building in Oklahoma City was bombed. That blast damaged buildings in a 16-block radius, where 168 people lost their lives, many of them children in the day care center, along with another 300+ injured. For the first time, I saw search and rescue dogs work in real time. It was the images of those children that pushed me forward toward my goal of training a SAR dog.

The next year I purchased a golden retriever from a breeder in Portland, Oregon, who bred dogs for many of the top SAR teams in the United States and abroad. Darlin (like the song "Oh my Darlin, you were lost and gone forever") was my first self-trained SAR dog. She was certified before the age of 2 and eventually was trained to find missing persons, locate cadavers, recover bodies underwater, and locate incinerated cadaver. After

Darlin passed, my oldest son and I trained an Australian shepherd, named Orion, who passed during the writing of this book, and another golden, named Draco, who now works as a therapy dog.

Along with training my own dogs, I also shared my training protocol with new dog handlers, who were struggling with a lack of training info. At one point I was contacted by a fire captain of the Chicago Fire Department to help work out problems with his dogs, who then responded to 9/11, and worked with police canine handlers when they felt they needed to sharpen their skill. In 2005 I retired from search and rescue, but continued with Draco as a therapy dog.

In 2012, I received an email from my son's childhood babysitter, who now was grown up with kids of her own. The message read:

"Hey stranger!

How are you? I have a doggie question for you. We are thinking about getting a puppy. I would like to train this new pup to alert to Collin's low blood sugar levels. I have been reading about the training, and to get a "real" diabetes alert dog costs nearly $20,000. I did find quite a few people online that successfully trained their own puppies to do this.

Do you have any thoughts, connections, suggestions, warnings? Collin is going to want to start staying home alone and I would feel so much better if we had a protective alert dog. Am I hoping for the impossible?

Thanks!!!"

I remember answering "no", telling her that it takes a lot of time to train a dog like that. I knew nothing about how diabetic alert dogs were trained, and recommended working with a breeder that knows something about diabetic alert dogs. I didn't hear from Kendra again for about three months, but then came another email informing me they got a real cute puppy named Ping (after the model of Collin's insulin pump) and wanted me to meet her. I still had no intention of training a diabetic alert dog, but agreed to meet the new little pup.

Before I went to meet Ping, curiosity got the best of me and I searched the internet for information about training a diabetic alert dog. I quickly found an assortment of blogs, message boards, and websites where parents told wonderful stories of how diabetic alert dogs changed their lives and were no longer wrought with fear over not catching when their child's blood sugar dipped too low or spiked too high. I also found questions about trying to train a diabetic alert dog and plenty of websites advertising trainers who would train them for a hefty fee.

What I couldn't find was a website with a comprehensive and step-by-step guide on how to train one yourself. I was shocked! Even when I started teaching myself how to train a search and rescue dog, I could find several books on search dogs to guide my training, but I couldn't find a single book on diabetic alert dogs. I quickly realized that maybe diabetic alert training wasn't so different from all the books and protocols about search and rescue training... instead of training the dog to find cadaver scent, you train for the scent of low blood sugar. All you would need is a dog with a strong play drive, a good nose, a strong bond with a type 1 diabetic, and nerves of steel (dog and the trainer alike).

Luckily for Kendra, Ping had incredible focus, a strong play drive, and was eager to learn. That night Kendra and I made a handshake agreement: we would try to train Ping on our own and record the process for other families who might want to train their own alert dog.

Since the start of Ping's journey, a couple of other books on diabetic alert dogs have been written, and I encourage you to read them. Read each one and educate yourself; the more knowledge you have the more equipped you will be. As you read this book I want you to remember I did not train Ping for them, as some of these paid trainers do. I only instructed Collin and Kendra how to go about training. We would meet weekly to discuss Ping's progress, Kendra would send videos through email, or she might text me a question about one of the drills. It was a lot of hard work, but it was all done by them at their own home. For me, it was so wonderful to be back training a dog and working with a child to teach them how smart and valuable dogs are. Whether you are like Kendra and want to train a diabetic alert dog in your home or like me and want to expand your knowledge of service dogs, I hope you enjoy our book and help spread awareness of diabetic alert dogs and type 1 diabetes.

-Shari Finger

Chapter 1- So you're thinking about training a D.A.D.?

A diabetic alert dog can be trained in the home, and it is possible to train him to be just as effective as one that was professionally trained. However, this is not for everyone. First of all, you must have a background in or knowledge of dog training. The perfect person is someone who has had dogs and has taken a dog through training in obedience, sports or other dog activities. You must love dogs and be the kind of person that enjoys having a dog with them every minute of the day! Training a diabetic alert dog is frustrating, time consuming, aggravating, endless, and sometimes doesn't work despite your effort. You may fail. Failure could mean that the dog you have picked is just not cut out to do this kind of work. But, more often it is the person who fails. So do your homework first; read this book and every book and website that you can find on training and diabetic alert dogs. Then, stick to one or a combination of sources which you understand and feel comfortable with.

What is a diabetic alert dog?

A diabetic alert dog (D.A.D.) is a canine trained to alert to low and high blood sugar in a human. An 'alert' is a term that the dog community uses to describe a behavior where a dog is trained to communicate through an action. Examples of common alerts are: barking, scratching, bumping, touching, or sounding an alarm. Diabetic alert dogs are trained to alert when they smell a chemical released into the saliva and sweat of a diabetic when their blood sugar levels are too low or high. Dogs have an incredible sense of smell due to their approximately 220 million olfactory cells, compared to a human's measly 5 million. This makes it possible for dogs to smell things we cannot.

Is a D.A.D. right for you?

Training and living with a D.A.D. is not easy. Before you run out and get a dog, do some serious soul searching to be sure it is the right thing for you. Here are some things to keep in mind:

- Do you have the money to properly take care of a dog? Your D.A.D. must be fed quality food. Food is fuel and your dog must be at peak health. An unhealthy D.A.D. may not have the energy to be on duty 24/7, and a good diet is essential to maintain energy levels.

- Veterinary care is also expensive and a D.A.D. must receive the best care possible. Training equipment and classes add up as well.

- Do you have the time to train a D.A.D.? It will start with an hour every day broken into four to six sessions for a puppy and will grow to 45-minute sessions three-to-four times a day.

- Do you have the discipline? If it's raining or snowing, you still have to train. You have to train with the patience of a saint and be able to keep it fun even when it isn't.

- Have you ever trained a dog? A person without dog training experience could follow the steps in a book successfully, but it is difficult without some help. If you have never stepped foot in an obedience class, you may want to contact a positive reinforcement trainer that understands your goal to train your own service dog and is willing to help you with the basics of dog training and obedience.

- Be prepared to take this dog everywhere and to be organized enough to have everything you need with you at all times. You'll need at least a leash, water, poop bags, water bowl, towel for muddy feet, food, and all your diabetic needs.

- You will spend a lot of time answering questions from curious people that see you with a dog and want to pet it. You won't be able to go anywhere without being stopped.

- Most of all, you really have to love dogs. This training will not work in a negative setting. You and your dog will be tied together for many years, so you need to enjoy being with your D.A.D.

Chapter 2- Kids and dogs

As a dog trainer, I love to work with children. My love for working with children and dogs stems from my own life experiences. I was one of those kids that loved dogs and wanted to keep each one I saw, which drove my parents batty. When I was 13 years old, I found and befriended a stray dog. This dog looked and acted like it had never lived in a house and ran from anyone who tried to catch her. Her ability to outrun even an Olympic athlete, eating anything that wouldn't eat her, and all the other bad habits were probably the skills that kept her alive out in the cruel and cold dog-eat-dog world.

Of course, in true dog-loving form, I begged my parents to keep the dog. I named her Pepsi, which quickly turned into the nickname Pepy. Pepy was truly a running machine. After several incidents of her slipping her collar, a trip to the local dog pound, and fines my parents had to pay (for a dog that wasn't even ours) they made me a deal. I could only keep Pepy if I took her to obedience school.

I took Pepy to school, and I was the only child among grown-ups. I listened to everything the instructor said and practiced at home to the point of obsessiveness. The last night of class had a test and, to my surprise, Pepy and I did great. I was so proud of her! I can still see her looking up at me in a perfect sit. But the true test of how well I taught Pepy came one day while visiting my grandparents. My grandmother opened the door to get the mail and Pepy reverted to old behavior by bolting out the door and down the street! She was gone and my grandmother could not run after her. She managed to yell, "PEPY, SIT!" imitating me as she had heard me practice a million times at her house. My grandmother says that Pepy skidded into the sit position. She walked up to her, grabbed her collar, and marched her into the house scolding her all the way.

Today when I work with children and their dogs, I always think of Pepsi and what I accomplished with that stray. I know that the child standing in front of me can accomplish the same thing. Most of all, I know what Pepy did for me. I wasn't the best in school, but I was good at training dogs and none of my friends could. I also gained a constant companion who I had until I was 26 years old and had children of my own. Simply put, children can train dogs, can make great dog trainers, and sometimes they listen better than adults.

Collin and Ping (3 months) practicing obedience.

Most kids say they want a puppy but have no idea of the responsibilities which go along with dog ownership. It has to be the parent that makes the decision whether or not to get the family a dog, and getting a puppy to train as a D.A.D. requires serious consideration. You need to be aware of the massive amount of time and dedication it takes to train a D.A.D. Working with your puppy, doing scent training and obedience several times every day on top of everything else you do with a type 1 diabetic child can be more than a person can handle.

D.A.D.s aren't right for every child. Keep in mind that their cooperation is essential to succeed in the type of training demonstrated in this book. Because the child plays a huge part in the training process, a child who has no interest in dogs or other issues, such as being afraid of dogs, should not be forced to work with a dog. This is not a good situation to put a dog in, and it will drive you, the chief dog trainer, up a wall. If this is the case, a professionally trained D.A.D. may be a better route.

If your child enjoys and is excited about dogs, they can significantly help with D.A.D. training. When I had my own children, they were very involved in the training of my search dogs. Our Australian shepherd search dog was trained solely by my oldest son, Jon, who was only 15 at the time. Can a child train a D.A.D. alone? Maybe, but probably not without some help from an adult. With this book, other books like this, and using your own brain to make it fit to you and your dog, it is possible. The D.A.D. may not be exactly like a professionally trained D.A.D., but they do not have to be. They just need to be consistently correct and have the ability to accurately alert.

As a parent, you must evaluate your child's ability and involvement in training a D.A.D. An older child can be the main trainer with your guidance or an assistant trainer working with you. With a younger child, you as the parent will do most of the work and involve the child at appropriate times. Because every person reading this book has a different situation, there is no way for me to say exactly what you need to do. But I hope to give you enough information that you will be able to make it work for you.

If your child loves animals, has that spark in their eye every time they get to hang out with the neighbor's dog, can take instruction, and is enthusiastic, then you are on the right track. As the parent you must be creative and find ways to make this fun and constructive all at the same time for both the child and dog. Kids have a marvelous way of training dogs.

Chapter 3- Picking a dog

Breeds

It does not matter if the dog you choose is a purebred or a mixed breed, but certain breeds are better for this type of work than others. Dogs with longer noses scent better than dogs with short noses. For example, a golden retriever would work better than a pug since the golden's nose is longer and has more olfactory cells. Some popular breeds to consider are labs, German shepherds, border collies, and golden retrievers.

Starting with a puppy

Not every dog has what it takes, so picking the right dog will be the single most important part of this process; everything rides on this one decision. Let's say you have a friend that has a litter of lab puppies, and you find yourself standing in the middle of a litter of puppies. With all the puppy chaos at your feet, how can you possibly know which one is the right one? For starters, you could download one of the many puppy intelligence and temperament tests from the internet and try to do it on your own. However, when I pick a puppy myself, I watch them very carefully over a period of weeks. I watch the puppies interact with each other and take each one away to play simple games with them.

But that's not how I did it in the past. I now have 30+ years in the dog community, and early on I would find a breeder that was on the same wavelength as me and had working knowledge of the type of dog I needed. Good breeders know the qualities of their dog's breed, their parents, and the puppies. No one knows those puppies better than a respectable breeder. The breeders are the puppy specialists; listen to their input. Here is a list of things to look for and think about when looking for a puppy:

1. Play Drive- Play drive is at the top of the list of qualities your little canine student needs to have. Watch not for the bully, but the one that plays hard and doesn't give up. Do not discount the puppy that stands to the side and watches from time to time and then joins back in the pile of puppies.

2. <u>Health</u>- Your D.A.D. must be healthy. Critical training time will be wasted if your puppy has health issues. It would be even worse if you train your D.A.D. and then it becomes ill and cannot work or its health affects the quality of his job. Your breeder must have impeccable standards for care including:

    a. Genetics- Tests of hips and eyes found on the pedigree for at least two generations
    b. Good nutrition -The breeder should be feeding top quality food
    c. Cleanliness- The puppies and the area where they live should be clean
    d. Veterinary Care- The appropriate shot and deworming should have been given according to their age (check with your vet on what should have been given when)

3. <u>Everyday Interactions</u>- It's important that the first 7+ weeks were spent in a loving environment with the puppy playing hard with his littermates and have been handled by the breeder. A good breeder has a list of things they do with a puppy before you even get them. A puppy that is ignored, not handled, not exposed to everyday experiences, or kept in a crate will not make a good service dog (or at least the odds will be against you). If you're not an experienced handler, then steer away from this situation.

4. <u>Problem Solving</u>- A puppy that naturally thinks through problems is a good candidate. Working out problems is another key quality your puppy will need.

5. <u>Attitude</u>- A friendly, non-aggressive nature is integral. A D.A.D. has to love people and react in a passive and positive way no matter how stressful the situation.

6. <u>Physically Active</u>- A D.A.D. is on the job 24/7 and needs to be healthy and active. A couch potato dog does not make a good D.A.D. because they will not have the energy level to be ready at all times.

7. <u>Capability to Learn and Stay Focused-</u> Most dogs can learn to learn, but for the best D.A.D.s the ability to learn is a natural trait. A dog with the ability to stay focused is an asset in dog training.

8. <u>Guts, Courage, Sass, Spunk-</u> A D.A.D. must have the courage and spunk to react and alert to a low or high blood sugar and never be intimidated by their surroundings. They need the attitude that they are always right and will walk through fire to do their job.

Rescuing a puppy

Ping was a rescue. Her litter was found on the side of the road in Illinois.

When rescuing a puppy, you lack the control and insight that you have when you get a puppy from a breeder. Yet, rescuing is a wonderful thing, and my favorite D.A.D., Ping, is a rescue. Unfortunately, the knowledge needed to make this decision is something I cannot teach you in this book. I am not even sure it's something that can be taught; it's something you learn from experience. If you do choose to get a rescue, consider finding someone with experience to help you make that decision.

Starting an older dog

You can teach an old dog new tricks. No dog is too old, but you may not want to go that route. It takes many hours to train a D.A.D., and you will want to get as many years of work from him. Starting out with a six year old limits the time he will be useful.

Starting with a six month, one year, or even a two year old is a possibility; if the dog has the right qualities, has been involved in training, and understands the learning process. For example, if you have a three year old shepherd living in your home and has done obedience classes, maybe some agility work, and seems to learn new things easily, he could be a candidate.

Should you choose a puppy or older dog?

Puppy- It is difficult sometimes to see the puppy's qualities by the time you need to decide to bring him home. How can you know for sure if this dog will grow up and have what it takes to be a D.A.D.? Let's imagine you spend the first couple of months living with a hyper, biting, pooping, peeing, and shredding machine only to find out he grew into a couch potato and doesn't like to play? Or maybe he could care less about treats and is impossible to motivate. Some of these qualities can be trained out, but it will be frustrating and add extra time to your training. The good news about these situations is at least you can start training away these problems immediately. With a puppy, compared to an older dog, you can train exactly the way you want and will not have to undo any previously learned unwanted behaviors. The most important benefit to getting a puppy is to create an unbreakable bond between the diabetic and the pup. Creating a solid puppy-person bond is essential; without it, your dog is just living in your house. When you have built a bond, your dog will know when you are turning the corner a block away and be waiting for you at the door. Any dog that has built a strong bond with a person always wants to please them, which makes training easier.

Older dog- An older dog is one that is no more than two years old. This may be a poor option because by the time he completes training the work years are limited. Also, if the dog didn't live with you before training there is no way to know if any bad behaviors have 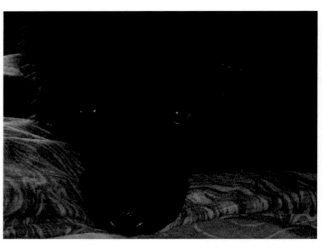 developed or if they are unsociable. You may find yourself spending a large amount of time undoing unwanted behaviors, instead of spending time building wanted ones. But a dog that has spent quality time with people and has been active in training may learn quickly and be ready for action in a reasonable amount of time.

When you start with a puppy, you may not be able to see if he or she is flawed, but you have a better chance to train in good behaviors and create a healthy bond. With an older dog, you can see the flaws but poor training may have created some unwanted behavior despite its increased focus and trainability. You can still create a strong bond with an older dog, but it's different from the one that you develop when you start working with a puppy. The choice is yours, but please make this decision carefully. Don't be afraid to ask for help. If you are picking a puppy, do the research and find a breeder with service dog experience. If they do not have a litter or a puppy in the litter that they feel will be a good candidate, then ask them to go with you to look at other litters. Any breeder that is professional will not have a problem going and looking at other pups. Breeders enjoy smart, educated dog owners, and if they know you are hiring them to pick the right dog, they will do it. Any older dog can be evaluated by a qualified trainer to see if they are a good candidate. Be sure to get a vet record and training information if this is a dog that is not already living in your home. If rescuing, be sure to talk to the foster home and get as much information as possible. If the dog is not in the foster system and has been in a cage for a long period, be very careful because this might not be the best candidate.

Multiple dogs in your home

Ping and Probie (12-year-old Labrador).

Chances are if you love dogs enough to think you can train your own D.A.D., then you probably have a dog in your home. Perhaps this dog is not suited for D.A.D. training for one of the reasons listed above. Whatever your reasons, you need to understand a couple things about having multiple dogs and training a D.A.D. First, different dogs can have different sets of rules. For example, the dog that lives in your house may not be allowed to go into the basement while your D.A.D. can and will need to freely go into all areas of your home. Situations like this often cause the human more distress than the dogs. As a human, we add emotions to situations.

Dogs don't experience emotion the same way we do. So when in the basement with your D.A.D., you might look up and see your other dog at the top of the stairs looking down at you with sad eyes. Remember: it is okay. Your dogs will get used to it and not hold a grudge.

Second, it is very difficult to work with more than one dog at a time. Sometimes, it almost seems like they are tag teaming you just to push you over the proverbial edge. I recommend only working with one dog at a time. Do not let the situation turn you into an angry and frazzled leader. As a leader, you always need to stay cool, under control, and not emotional.

Lastly, it may be better if your D.A.D. is the only dog in the home. It is very important that your world revolves around the diabetic and the D.A.D. With more than one dog in the home, a bond will always form between the dogs. This is risky as the bond between dogs may be stronger than the bond between D.A.D and diabetic. Sometimes, the other dogs can even be a distraction and your D.A.D. may not be able to do his job. Do people with D.A.D.s have multiple dogs? Yes. It can be done, but be aware that it will come with additional challenges.

Chapter 4- Dog training basics

Ground rules

- Food should never be given from the table or just to be nice. D.A.D.s are working dogs and should learn to earn their food and treats.

- All family and close friends must be on the same page in regards to training. Explain the plan to family members and friends who will come in contact with your little student. If someone doesn't understand the importance of what you're are trying to accomplish, then they should not interact with your D.A.D. Every time someone breaks the rules it sets you back in your training.

- Train consistently.

- Control everything: playing, feeding, and even pooping.

- Keep it happy. If you are not in the mood or the dog is acting wacky, then skip training and just play and interact with your dog (see the section on games that also teach).

- Socialize your puppy with similar aged puppies. However, make sure to limit socialization after one year (see next chapter).

- The person with diabetes should talk to the D.A.D.-in-training all the time. Have him or her tell the puppy about their day or what they want for dinner.

- Maintain good nutrition. We have many choices for quality dog food now. Stick with ingredients from the US and not from other countries. Consult your vet, breeder, or better yet do some research and become an expert.

- Take your D.A.D. everywhere. Get him familiar to all situations.

- Do not restrict where your D.A.D. is allowed. It doesn't matter if you just had new carpeting installed in the family room and don't want your dog on it. You made a commitment to have a D.A.D., and your dog needs to be able to travel freely throughout your home. The D.A.D. must be allowed up on things like couches and chairs, as they may need to jump up and get closer to get a better sniff. Your D.A.D. needs to be able to do his job in every inch of your home.

8 Simple tips to be a GREAT dog trainer

The puppy isn't the only one who has to learn. A good D.A.D. comes from a good trainer, so it's just as important for you to learn to train as it is for them to learn to sniff.

1. <u>Learn to use your voice.</u> You should be able to make your dog squirm on the floor out of happiness by just hearing your voice. Most people raise their pitch and act a little silly. You also should be able to stop any behavior with one sound. I use a loud "ahh", some say "out", and other famous trainers say "Shhhhh!" with a snap of the fingers.

2. <u>Reward and mark at the magic moment.</u> There is a special moment when a dog successfully completes a command when you must reward them. The more times you hit that magic moment, the faster your dog will learn and remember what he learned. Imagine you command your dog to sit in front of you, and the dog starts to move into position. As soon as his butt touches the ground (which is the *magic moment*) you should say "yes!" (called the *mark*) and extend your hand with a treat. Always praise your

dog verbally by saying something like "Good girl!" in a happy voice (after the mark) so your dog relates praise to the food reward.

3. Always do everything the same way. Say the same thing and use the same body language every time. When you go to walk or heel your dog hold the leash the same way: have your dog walk on your left side, sit on your left side, and then give the command heel and step out with your left foot (the foot closest to your dog). Even changing minor things every day leads to less consistency in learning.

4. There is no place for emotion in dog training. A person that gets angry, frustrated, impatient, or overreacts to situations is not a good dog trainer. It is essential to stay calm and cool at all times.

5. Training sessions need to be like a game. You need the same motivation to train as your dog has when he sees you pick up a tennis ball.

6. Train many times a day and in short sessions. Keeping sessions short will keep your dog fresh and focused. Allowing a training session to go on too long can frustrate both dog and handler. Keeping the session short ensures that the dog stays focused throughout the lesson. If you trained your dog at every commercial break while you watch TV, then your dog would be the best dog in the neighborhood. No matter how short, make sure to end the session on a positive note.

7. Never punish unless you catch your dog in the act. Dogs live in the moment and will not connect the crime to the punishment if you don't catch them in the act. Do NOT punish your dog by putting them in a time out, by hurting them, or staying mad more than a moment. Dogs don't play mind games. They don't do things like chew up your shoe because they are mad at you for working overtime or petting the neighbor's dog. It simply doesn't work like that. Be very careful of when and how to punish.

How do dogs learn

Dogs are smarter than we give them credit for. I've seen dogs find bodies underwater, travel miles following the scent of one particular person while ignoring the other 35 people, and give comfort to a brain cancer patient in hospice care. To be a good teacher you have to understand the process they use to learn these amazing skills. Remember: all dogs are not the same and you are guaranteed to run into problems. So long as you understand how a dog learns, you should be able to think through the training problem.

- Dogs can learn from other dogs. If you have another dog in the house, it can help with housebreaking. Be cautious though, this is a double-edged sword; they can pick up bad habits, like barking at squirrels passing through the yard.

- Dogs learn by guided movement. This does not mean forcing the rear quarters down to sit or pushing them flat to go into a down. Instead, use a treat to draw them into position or using body language to promote a particular movement. Think of it this way: a dog will learn faster if you get their brain to produce the movement which fulfills the command. As an example, have your dog stand in front while you hold a treat in your hand. Take said treat and, starting at their face, move it over their nose to their forehead. The dog will need to look up to see it and will sit down to do so. This is how you can teach a movement command by guiding your dog.

- Dogs act in the moment- not by reminiscing on the past. *Capturing* is when you catch a dog in mid-action and reward the behavior to encourage repeating that behavior. Example: when your dog wakes up from a nap you notice that he always stretches and it resembles him bowing. So for a fun trick you want to teach him to bow on command. You wait until he awakes from his next nap, and when he goes to stretch you say "bow!" and reward him. Your dog will quickly learn that this action always gets a reward. Capturing is taking an already established behavior and marking it with a command without actually having to teach it.

- Like humans, dogs learn through repetition. Once your dog successfully completes a new command, repeat the command several times in a row. However, be sure not to overdo it. Always quit before your dog gets bored, tired, or loses interest. Make sure to end on a positive note. I once had a trainer tell me that if your dog does it seven times in a row successfully then they will always remember it. As a trainer, I see that repeating a command with positive reinforcement and correct timing (hitting that magic moment in #3) turns your dog into a quick learner.

Training log

Keeping a log of training details is very important. However, it is time consuming and can be easily forgotten in the hustle and bustle of D.A.D. training life. Still, I emphasize the importance of ALWAYS keeping a log for the following reasons:

- It tracks each exercise practiced and the result.

- It keeps you on track and focused toward training goals.

- It documents the learning process, which will allow you to analyze your training process and make changes to become more efficient.

- If your dog starts to have difficulties in completing a training goal, you can look back in your training log and not rely on memory.

- It allows you to see patterns, such as locations where your D.A.D. doesn't perform as well or certain blood sugar levels which might need more practice.

What should be included in your log?

Your training log should include details that will be beneficial to future training. It also documents the amount of time spent training, which can be used as proof if you are ever questioned about your service dog's training. Regardless, if you use the format in this book, you should consider including the following:

1. Each training session should include the date, time, location, and age of the dog (to chart progression).

2. Include all obedience work. Record commands given, how many times, how many were successful, and if you had problem getting a response to a command then give a brief description of what happened.

3. When doing scent work, always record the blood sugar number.

4. And, as you go along, record any extra details that may be important to you. For example, I had a student who kept track of which treats seemed to be more of a motivator.

Here you will find a sample template training log that you can photocopy or use as inspiration.

SCENT TRAINING LOG

Date_____   Low or High   Scent Sample #

Location_____

Carrier _____

Time to tell _____

Time to alert _____

Notes:_____
_____
_____
_____
_____

Notes should include distance the scent had to travel to target, if outside, up wind or downwind, dogs attitude, etc.

Obedience classes

Service dogs, which includes D.A.D.s, must be well mannered at all times. There are no exceptions to this! In my opinion, it will be harder and take longer to teach you dog good manners than to teach them to alert to high and low blood sugar. You will need to find a trainer or obedience classes for you to attend with your dog. If you have gone to classes in the past, maybe even trained a couple of dogs, it is still a good idea to go to dog class. I always go back to dog class with a puppy, even though I also have taught the class. Obedience class teaches discipline for both you and your dog by making you go every week, and also produces a good doggy work ethic. Dogs love to work and they will enjoy going to class, which will develop into the behavior that is needed in public.

Be sure and pick an excellent obedience program. Ideally, find someone that has knowledge of service work and understands what makes a good D.A.D. But, more than likely that will not be the case. You will have to use a little of your gut instinct when deciding. You want to find a program where there are multiple levels, starting out with puppy class and moving forward as your dog matures in age and knowledge. Be sure they teach all the traditional dog commands.

As a starting point, I am a fan of the Canine Good Citizen Program offered by the American Kennel Club. You can go to their site and contact an evaluator in your area and get a recommendation from them. Always ask if you can visit a couple of classes before you sign up to be sure that they are a good fit for your needs. Your trainer should use positive reinforcement and keep it fun.

Warning signs

Dog training has changed immensely over the last 15 years. Certain methods of training obedience are not right for a D.A.D. Some warning signs of bad training will be trainers that use choke collars or intimidation. Be wary of trainers that put a choke or prong collar on all the dogs in class. All dogs do not need these types of collars and one should not be used on a D.A.D. Do not work with a trainer that uses this equipment for every dog regardless of temperament. Poor trainers also use intimidation. People that scream, hit, slam your dog to the ground to show who is alpha, tell you if your dog is digging to fill the hole with water and hold their head into the water so they can't breathe, or leave the dog for hours as punishment is NOT a good trainer. All of these are examples of animal abusers!

Here is a real example of the aggressive training and trainers you should avoid. I liked to take my search and rescue dogs to agility class as it helped me with control when working off lead (air scenting search dogs need to be free to roam while working). There, I could introduce my dog to shaky surfaces, like the dog walk and teeter totter. Perhaps more importantly, search and rescue work can be stressful and this was a great way to have fun and blow off steam.

A local dog club rented a warehouse close to my home, and I was ecstatic that I could practically walk there instead of attending my regular class that was almost an hour away. My son and I each took one of our dogs and, to our surprise, the training techniques used were unfathomable! The instructor handled some of the shy or unsure dogs by dragging them over obstacles, yelling at them, correcting them by jerking them by their leash, or yanking and twisting their collars. My blood pressure went sky high every night. I held my tongue until our dog Orion, a young Australian shepherd, was going through an obstacle course and became distracted by someone sitting on the sidelines. For some reason Orion blew off the next obstacle and went to visit. My son Jon ran up and got Orion and started over and at the same exact spot, but Orion did it again. The instructor told the person that if our dog broke his command again, they needed to yell and stomp their feet in an effort to make sure he would never want to visit a person on the sidelines again. I not-so-calmly went over to the instructor and told her we were leaving because a search and rescue dog can never be afraid to approach anyone. I wasn't about to let her undo all of our training with her kooky techniques. The moral of the story is that you need to be sure that everyone who comes into contact with your D.A.D.-in-training is a positive influence. Don't be afraid to change things if something doesn't feel right. A D.A.D. is not a machine and they can't work if they are afraid of the people around them.

Who should take the puppy to obedience class?

A D.A.D. is always in training, and you will always be honing their skills. The person that is responsible for the dog's behavior should be the one to attend class. Even though dog training is hard work, it is also very rewarding and can be a great way to relieve stress. The relationship you develop with the dog you train is special. Dogs have a magical way of making you feel better; they are always ready to listen when you need to talk. If your child is young, you as the parent or caretaker, should take the dog to obedience class. An older child is definitely capable of doing the obedience training as long as they follow the rules and take it seriously.

Another option is to do what we did. Collin was 10 years old when we started. When they first got Ping, Collin did all the obedience work. Collin learned how to deliver a command and reward correctly. He also understood all the commands and what was expected. Collin spent his entire summer vacation training Ping, which built a strong bond between them. When Collin went back to school, Kendra and I started working with Ping and included Collin whenever he wasn't playing baseball. This worked well because for the first couple of months Ping was in that cute puppy stage. But, like every dog in the world, some days you wake up and it seems as if they forgot everything you taught them, and the only cure for that is a firm dog handler. Even though we took Collin out of the obedience part of the training, he was still involved in the scent training, and he and I started doing agility with Ping, which put Collin back in the driver seat.

Training techniques to teach children

Ping (4 months) waiting for Collin to deliver a command.

If the child with type 1 diabetes is old enough to help you train your D.A.D., you will want to encourage them to deliver a command with confidence. Be sure the child says it loud enough for the dog to hear and with a sharp (but not mean or mad sounding) voice. The child needs to learn how to use their voice. The same goes for rewarding the dog with praise. The child should be able to change their voice to a happy tone that makes it clear to the dog that the child approves. While a command is given with meaning, the child should always stay calm. I discourage rough housing between you, your puppy, and your child because the puppy may start to view the child more like a playmate than a leader. However, puppies do need to be puppies and play to stay mentally balanced, but for puppy-D.A.D.s, scent work training is their form of play.

Teaching the basics between puppy and child

Being able to deliver a command will only work if your child knows how to deliver the reward. There are several ways you can teach your child to give a treat. Teaching your child how to handle treats before you are actually in a training situation will reduce confusion for both the child and dog.

Cora (Collin's sister) rewarding Ping for completing a command.

Treat and release- This is a simple game that reinforces important skills in both the dog and the child. Release the treat at the exact moment the command is completed. Verbally praise your dog so they relate the completion of the command to the food and praise. Eventually, the food reward can be eliminated and the dog only praised for a job well done.

The nibble- This is when the handler holds a treat between their fingers and lets the dog nibble on it without actually giving it to the dog. This technique is used to keep a dog in place and focused on the treat. Teaching your child how to control the dog and keep it focused on the reward comes in handy.

The dog magnet- This is similar to 'the nibble', but has a different goal. Hold a small treat between your thumb and index finger tightly and place it directly in front of your puppy's nose. Let them smell and lick but not eat it. You can use this to move your dog from one place to another, just like the proverbial carrot-on-a-string. Let us say that I want to move my puppy away from my side to the front where she can sit. This may seem simple, but puppies might be confused by this command at first. To maneuver the puppy, take a treat and use it like a magnet and lure her to the exact spot where she should sit. Once she arrives at the right spot, release the treat. The lure method is used all the time in dog training. It is an effective method to teach instead of pulling, carrying, or yelling. Eventually, you will be able to pinch your fingers together (without the treat) and have them move the same way using praise when the puppy arrives at the intended place.

The tail wag game- Have your child repeat simple phrases like "What a good puppy!" in the happiest voice they can make. You can also have them make kissing noises or any other silly sound that the puppy seems to like. Without using their hands, and only using their voice, encourage the child to try and get the dog to wag its tail and come. The faster the wag the better.

The "Come!" game- The come command is often the weakest command for most dogs despite its importance. Start the game just a couple of feet away from your puppy and have the child deliver the "Come!" command with that tail wag voice (see 'tail wag game', above). When commanding your dog, always use a happy voice. When the dog comes to the child, have the child use their tail wag voice and praise the pup and give a treat (using 'treat and release', as shown above). Encourage everyone to call the dog in this manner and always use the dog's name first and then "Come!" Dogs learn their names quickly and by saying the name before the command you get their attention. Once the dog happily runs to the child every time you say "[name], come!" you are ready to go on. Have the child move farther away and work their way up to calling from other rooms. You can even have other family members join in and have the dog run from room to room when given the "Come!" command. If your dog doesn't run toward the child at the start, have the child walk backward while calling the puppy. When you back up, the dog will be more likely to come (it's a dog thing) and come faster.

Mark and reward- In this game, the mark, as mentioned before, is the vocal reinforcement and the reward is the treat. The goal is to have the child practice a command and mark, or vocally reinforce, the puppy at that magic moment (the exact moment the command is completed). Children can learn to mark as easily as adults. For example, if I tell my dog to "Sit!" he will start to move into the sitting position. The magic moment, where I should mark, is the exact moment her butt touches the ground, thus completing the "Sit!" command. To mark, I use a loud and happy "Yessss!" At the same time, my hand is extending toward the dog to give them a treat. This is the reward. Make sure that the treat is already in your hand before the command and you are not struggling to get a treat out of your pocket while your pup already forgets what he has just done. At first, both you and the child should mark together so they learn how to do it- it takes practice and you should both be doing it similarly.

Socializing

Ping socializing with Collin and Cora's cousin, Mackenzie.

Your goal for socializing will be to introduce your puppy to five new people per day. Always be sure that the person you introduce them to is a confident positive dog person. To properly introduce your D.A.D., give the sit command before the person starts to pet them. Once your D.A.D. is sitting and calm, then the new person can pet your dog. If the puppy or dog tries to stand, make sure the petting stops until they sit again. Your D.A.D. has to be confident and respectful when meeting new people.

If the puppy seems nervous and fearful, try these tips to work through it:

- Choose dog friendly people (dogs can sense this).

- Have the person kneel down, avoiding direct eye contact. Encourage the dog to smell the new person.

- Have the person slowly extend their hand with a treat (repeat several times).

- For the extremely squeamish puppy, ask your new person to kneel on the floor while not making eye contact. Have them gently toss treats towards the puppy and gradually reduce the distance with each toss until the dog chooses to move close to get the treat. Eventually, the puppy should warm up to the person; sometimes it's in the same session, other times it may take days. When the dog gets pretty comfortable picking up treats on the floor close to you, graduate to slowly extending your hand with a treat in it while continuing not to make eye contact. You can also try setting the treat on your knee or lap and allowing the dog to pick up the treat.

Socializing with other dogs

Ping learning to be social with Draco, a therapy dog.

When you are out in the community, you will constantly run into other dogs. Some may be friendly, others may not be. Your D.A.D. must be able to ignore the other dogs and focus on his job. The answer is not to keep your dog away from the other dogs so they don't react, but to introduce them to other dogs so they are not fearful and interacting with other dogs becomes common place.

The proper way to have new dogs meet

1. Never allow dogs to meet off lead. If you have ever had to break up a dog fight you'll understand why this is important. When dogs fight it is loud, scary, and complete mayhem. It is a natural instinct to stop them so no one gets hurt, but without the leashes to pull them apart you will be forced to reach in and you will be bitten. Your dog won't realize it is you when fighting. It only knows that it's under attack, and it has to defend itself or die.

2. Try not to let dogs walk straight at each other. In the dog world that can be viewed as an attack and give off wrong signals. Try letting them approach each other from the sides; even better would be letting them meet nose-to-butt and then vice versa.

3. Do not pull your dog's lead tighter. Trainers always say that tight leads breed aggression in a dog. This means a dog at the end of a tight lead has a different mindset. If your dog is so out of control that you can't walk up to another dog in a calm and respectful way, then he shouldn't be meeting other dogs.

4. You may ask the question at some point, "Why am I letting my service dog meet other dogs when I don't want my dog to look at another dog and get ideas of playing? Their job is to ignore other dogs and pay attention to the diabetic!" There are two important reasons. First, if you don't let them meet other dogs at a young age, there is a possibility your dog could become fearful of other dogs, and fearful dogs often act aggressive. The second reason is that dogs learn proper doggie manners from each other and it is something they can only learn from each other. A dog that is sheltered from things, whether it's people, other dogs, loud noises, bikes, wheelchairs, cars, or squirrels can become fearful when confronted with them while doing their jobs. This fear can distract your D.A.D. and even make him totally ineffective. The best way to try to assuage that type of behavior is to expose your D.A.D. to everything and always keep it a positive experience.

5. If you're having a problem finding a dog for your puppy to play with, try contacting your local big pet supply store and see if they offer puppy

playtime. Many of them encourage customers to bring in puppies to socialize and of course it also gives them the opportunity to sell you obedience classes. Most of the time, you don't have to buy the lessons and puppy playtime is usually a free offer. If you casually mention to them that you are training a service dog, most times they would love to assist you by arranging a playmate. If they don't offer puppy playtime, then spend some time shopping around the store and sooner or later you will run into other puppies. Another trick is to look at the training schedule to see when they are offering puppy training and just show up around the same time to catch the puppies walking in or leaving the training.

The above works when you want your puppy to meet a friend, but what about dogs that may not want to meet your puppy? When out in public, be aware of other dogs and watch their behavior as they approach. You should be able to know whether to avoid them or to safely walk by through their body language. For example: I am walking with my D.A.D and perhaps I see a handler approaching and is dragging their dog along. In this case I would move over out of the way or even turn another in direction to avoid that encounter. But, if I see a dog and handler approach in a calm heel position then I am then confident that the dog is trained and the handler is a responsible dog owner.

Tips for puppy play

- Make sure each introduction is positive, so pick their playmate carefully. If something makes you uncomfortable, find a new playmate.

- When your puppy is 7 to about 14 weeks, keep playing to puppies only- no big dogs. Puppies haven't learned the signals that older dog use to control social situations. By playing with dogs of the same age, your puppy will learn those signals naturally from others.

- The puppy play will seem frantic and you will be standing there watching your little fur ball and thinking "This can't be good." It is good! It creates balance. When trainers talk about balance, it means allowing them to live in the world in which they were meant to live. Dogs are pack animals and when they are with a mentally healthy pack it is similar to an attitude adjustment or grounding.

- When puppies play, it may seem like they are going to hurt each other and it is hard to know when to stop them. Once in a while, someone may catch a tooth or get a little rough and a puppy may yipe. As long as they correct the behavior themselves, all is good. But if there is bullying, separate the puppies for a minute and let them play again once they settle down.

Chapter 5- Safety

The first step toward D.A.D. safety is to crate train your puppy. Crating is important and will help with house training, keeping your puppy safe when you can't watch them, and it gives your puppy a safe haven. Place the dog crate in the bedroom with the diabetic, if possible. If your puppy is keeping you awake at night or needs to be closer to the door for house training purposes, you can place it in a quiet place. Eventually, it will need to be moved into the diabetic's bedroom once they acclimate to your home. Once your puppy is comfortable in the house and is house broken, you can move them into the room with the diabetic and encourage for them to sleep as close to their head as possible.

You should always make going into the crate fun. Put your dog in their crate with a positive attitude and never when you are mad. Do not use the crate to punish your puppy for bad behavior. The crate is NOT a time out place. It is your dog's safe place to sleep or chill. Consider giving a nice healthy treat or a safe bone that will not splinter or break (not rawhide bones). My favorite is a rubber cone toy with a thin layer of peanut butter inside. Your puppy will exhaust himself licking every last little bit out and you can wash them in the dishwasher. Also mark the action of going into the crate with a command. For example, I say "Go crate!" or "Home!" You can say anything, but always say the same thing.

Ping asleep in her crate.

You know crate training is going well when you're getting ready to go out and just when you would say "Go crate!" your puppy jumps the gun and runs happily to the crate before the command. Another sign of successful crate training is if you find your puppy napping or lounging in the crate with the door still open.

In addition to crate training, you should puppy-proof your house to make sure it is safe for your puppy. Make sure there are not any exposed wires or small items that could be swallowed or chewed. Be sure all cabinets are secured so the puppy can't get into them. Also, keep all dangerous chemicals out of the dog's reach. Do not burn heavily scented candles or use room deodorizers. This is to protect your dog's nose by preventing exposure to synthetic odors.

A lesson learned

Because your D.A.D. is always out and about with you, they will come in contact with things that could hurt them. Anything from spoiled food, drugs, fertilizers, bug killer... the list is endless. You never know what is around the next corner. Ping was two months into her D.A.D. training and doing very well. Kendra, Collin, and I would meet at a park and work on obedience, and when we were finished we would sit in the grass and review our progress on scent training while watching Collin play on the playground. Kendra would constantly extract twigs, cigarette butts, and anything else Ping would get into her mouth. She was always very careful not to allow Ping to ingest anything. But, Ping was at that age where she wanted to chew on everything.

Because this had become an issue, I decided to move our training sessions to a different park. I picked a park that wasn't as busy and once we arrived we realized that this park would work out better than we had even imagined. It had a pavilion with a cement floor, and best of all it was clean. We had a great training session that night and ended with our usual review of the week while watching Ping and Collin play soccer together.

We said our goodbyes around 6 PM and Kendra and Collin met Cora and Dave, Collin's sister and father, at their Grandmother's for a family dinner. Around 9 o'clock I received a text from Kendra saying they were on the way to the vet, Ping was really sick. According to Kendra, after arriving home that night, Ping was relaxing on the front porch with her while she watched the kids play and enjoy the summer evening. When Ping got up to follow Dave out into the yard she walked like she was drunk and then laid down in the yard. They took Ping into the house, and she still couldn't walk so they packed up the kids and took off to the vet. The vet asked repeatedly if she had gotten into anything and if someone could have slipped her alcohol. They knew that there was no chance that Ping could be fed or even accidently got into alcohol that night because there wasn't any alcohol present. We thought through that night's training, thinking about every single thing that Ping did that night, and came up with no cause.

The vet wanted to keep Ping overnight to give fluids (that was a very hot day but we did give Ping water several times while training) and to keep her under observation. Kendra called me and said she wanted to bring Ping home since she could take better care of her all night at home. Previously, I had an experience with an accidental poisoning of my beloved dog Draco and knew how serious the situation was! Ping was only a couple of months old and the vet couldn't do anything without knowing what she had ingested. I told Kendra that she needed to leave Ping there and take the kids home, and deep down I know she knew that too. I couldn't think of anything worse than Ping dying at home in front of Collin.

I laid in bed that night thinking about how special Ping was and wondering how Collin would handle this. We surely couldn't start another dog for a while, and the bigger question was how we would ever find another Ping (in Collin's eyes). I fell asleep that night thinking about the day's events and if she wasn't poisoned then perhaps it was neurological. I knew that a dog with health issues could not be a D.A.D.

Kendra called the vet several times during the night and in the morning was told to come get their dog. We never did figure out what happened to Ping that night. The only explanation that we can possibly hang our hat on was that Ping was given a tick and flea preventive within 24 hours of this episode. It wasn't a common tick and flea ointment, it was a new one on the market and given by the veterinarian's office. When Kendra thought that it could be a possibility she looked up the company on the internet and to her surprise found complaints that the product had made dogs sick. To date, Ping continues to be a healthy and happy dog! The moral is to always protect your D.A.D.'s health and safety- everything from ingesting toxins, inhaling synthetic odors, to dog attacks!

Collin holding Ping in the veterinary office after she had to spend the night.

D.A.D.s around the house

Take your D.A.D. everywhere in the house to be sure he is familiar with their new home. Do not carry your D.A.D. around the house to expose them. Make sure all four of your puppy's feet are on the ground and let him investigate and safely explore his surroundings on his own.

Your D.A.D. needs to freely travel everywhere the diabetic does. Do not keep them out of the living room because you just got new carpet. If you're ever going to expect your D.A.D. to work there, do not restrict them now. If you start off restricting you may get a hesitation or refusal if the D.A.D. needs to enter to do his job and save a life! Your D.A.D. cannot understand a circumstance where he is not allowed to enter that room except when signaling low blood sugar. It simply doesn't work that way.

Your puppy should walk around the house with confidence and enter every room not being fearful of slippery floors, bathtubs, or the sound of the garage door going down. If he is fearful of something, try playing fun games in there or around the noise. The idea is to expose him to the thing he is afraid of while doing fun things so he relates the scary thing to something fun. Most puppies hit a fearful stage (starting *around* 12-14 weeks). Keep it positive and fun while calmly and confidently exposing him to his fear. Do not stop in the middle to pet, carry, hug, or kiss him. Service dogs need to learn to work through fear. He needs to see it like a dog on the floor, get to the other side, and see that it wasn't anything to fear.

For example, my dog is afraid of the clothes dryer buzzing when it is finished. If every time the dryer buzzed you stop what you are doing in a panic to pick up your dog, hug him, and tell him its ok, you are actually reinforcing their fear. But if you time it and play your dog's favorite game near the laundry room when it buzzes, and you don't acknowledge the noise then your dog will learn that fun things happen even though that scary noise happens.

A puppy's precious nose

Cora and Ping doing the "nose bump."

Be aware of your surroundings and protect your puppy's nose from fumes and harsh synthetic odors, such as candles and room fresheners. Extensive long term exposure to candles, air fresheners, etc. could hamper the puppy's ability to detect a low in the home. So use your candles sparingly, and don't take a needless risk.

Traveling with your D.A.D.

Ping and her travel bag.

Traveling with a dog or child is challenging enough, but traveling with a D.A.D. and a child with type 1 diabetes is extremely challenging. Figure out a system that works for you so you can carry food, water, treats, a poop bag, and whatever else you might need.

- Practice safe travel by securing your dog while in your car- use a tie down or seat belt. Never secure your dog by his collar.

- If you take public transportation or travel by foot, your D.A.D. can wear a service vest, allowing him to carry some necessities.

- Be sure to always have fresh water. Find an effective way to carry clean water at all times and bring an appropriate container, depending on if your dog will drink out of a bowl or a bottle.

- It's against the law in most communities to have your dog off lead. If not on lead, you could find yourself liable for injuries or damage caused by your D.A.D.

- Your D.A.D should be attached to the diabetic at all times. Scents travel via air currents and you need to have the D.A.D. as close to the source as possible.

- Service dogs that work in public should never be free to approach people and must be under control at all times. I run into people all the time that think that they are super trainers or that their dogs are so well trained that they don't need to be on lead. Well, they're wrong! I have seen the best trained dogs blow off commands for a squirrel. You have made an investment in your dog and should love them beyond words; you should not risk harm coming to them. You do not want your D.A.D. to dart out in front of a car or find you and your D.A.D. in the middle of a dogfight. You have a better chance of controlling the situation when your dog is on a leash.

- Never take your dog to places you are not welcomed when training. Just because you are training a service dog doesn't mean you have the right to go to places where dogs aren't normally welcomed before they are ready. There are many wonderful places where dogs are welcomed that in the past weren't available to us. Many coffee shops and restaurants have outdoor seating. Pet stores, malls, sporting goods stores, and home improvement chains often welcome dogs. Utilize places where you are welcomed for training and be sure your dog has good manners before you attempt more difficult situations.

- NO DOG PARKS! Your dog's fun comes from playing with you- not other dogs that could be aggressive or carry disease. It is good to socialize with other dogs but do it with dogs and handlers you know. I like to go to a big pet store and walk around. Not many people take their out of control dog to walk around a store. Usually, the dogs there are very well behaved and the handlers who are walking them have trained them and understand the unwritten rules of dog meetings and greetings.

- Four on the floor! Do not carry your dog around. They need to see the world from below and not from the penthouse view from your arms.

- A D.A.D. needs to have nerves of steel and be comfortable in all situations. By exposing your puppy to noises and experiences they will have to face in the future, you will make them grow into a sound and secure service dog. If you keep your little bundle of fur at home safe and sound till training takes you out into the big noisy dog world, your dog may be startled by noises, movement of other dogs, or people stopping and greeting. They need to spend every moment learning and understanding the outside world- not hiding from it.

Service vests

Service dogs often wear service vests allowing them to be identified by the public. However, the vest is more than just a visual ID. Start early in your dog's training by putting on their service vest in the morning or before you leave the house. Your dog will get comfortable wearing the vest and will not be distracted by it. Service vests also help in other ways, such as:

- Your dog will associate wearing the service vest with working. This means when you put the vest on, your D.A.D. will know it's time for business.

- It can save you from people stopping to pet your puppy. Most of the public understands that service dogs are working and should not be interrupted.

- You can get a vest with pockets and let your dog carry your blood sugar meter, glucose tablets, and other essentials. This also works well at home. Simply have everything you would need for a low blood sugar event packed in their vest. That way, when the diabetic doesn't feel good, they can have the D.A.D. "Come!" without having to move themselves.

Ping sporting her training vest and Ping learning to tolerate the service vest.

Chapter 6- Bonding

A bond between child and dog should be like imaginary handcuffs.

Your D.A.D. will need to bond with the diabetic. A dog that is devoted and loves to be with their person is more likely to be in nose range when needed. You must concentrate on building the bond between human and their dog.

The bond has to be based on joy. It is not about dominance, being alpha, or any of those other terms you hear so often when researching dog training. It is actually very simple. A happy, balanced, and bonded dog works for his person flawlessly. A scared and unhappy dog that has been beaten or yelled at into submission cannot work out simple problems or move beyond boundaries without confronting his fear. Scared dogs are more likely to miss important cues.

There are many things you can do to improve your bond. First, talk to your D.A.D. Talking to a dog keeps them in tune to you. It also keeps their mind working and stimulates curiosity. Having your dog get accustomed to your everyday emotional ups and downs as reflected in your voice, will allow the puppy to detect a change in your voice when in trouble. Second, spend quality time with your dog. Go on long walks and devote time to playing and enjoying your dog.

Ping waiting for Collin to come out of school.

A dog with a strong bond will always "know" when that person is coming.

Children and bedtime

Collin with Ping encouraging her to sleep near him.

Depending on the age of your puppy, you may want to start out with crating your puppy at night (see Chapter 5- Safety); both for your puppy's own safety and so everyone can get a good night sleep. If you're starting off with a very young dog, I suggest starting with a crate at night and concentrate on house training and sleeping through the night without barking or crying. Once you have achieved nighttime bliss, you can move the crate into the child's room. It seems to work best for everyone if this is done in transition. Even though your puppy has been sleeping through the night, he now has to learn how to wake up and go back to sleep.

Every time you walk into the room to check blood sugar levels, the puppy should wake up and when you leave he or she should quietly go back to sleep. If the child is low, the puppy should be let out to smell the natural low by cuddling and getting a yummy treat. This may sound odd, but remember that every time your puppy smells a low blood sugar event it should become happy party-time to positively reinforce the smell of low blood sugar. Once your puppy gets in the groove and isn't chewing up beloved stuffed animals, you can let them out of the crate and encourage them to sleep as close to the child's mouth as possible. This is not an easy task. There will be many long nights before the puppy learns that as soon as the light goes off it's time to be quiet even after a happy celebration of low blood sugar levels. I actually think this is more difficult than teaching a puppy to identify low blood sugar... so hang in there. It could be a bumpy ride!

Chapter 7- The alert

An **alert** is a signal that your dog gives you to tell you that the diabetic is dangerously low or high. I like to think of it as an alarm; and personally, I have a different opinion of what the alert should be than most professional D.A.D. and service dog trainers. I believe that D.A.D.s can be trained by non-professionals, that every dog's ability to learn is different, and an individual trainer's time, knowledge, and dedication may vary. Thus, it is better to avoid alerts that are complicated with multiple steps, and instead use simple alerts that can be accurate and dependable. It is my goal to give you enough information so you can make the right decision on which alerts will work best for you and your D.A.D.

I believe the alert should be an alarm that is the dog equivalent to a human jumping up and down with their arms in the air like you are flagging down help on a highway while screaming at the top of your lungs, "THIS KID'S BLOOD SUGAR IS LOW!! DANGER!!" I feel if you are going to train a dog to alert to something important as low blood sugar, which can kill, it should be an in your face obvious, unquestionable, and solid action.

An alert can be almost anything that changes the behavior of your dog enough that you can clearly identify it as the alert without doubt. Keep in mind that this is my personal feeling on the subject. First, make sure it is something you will actually be able to teach your dog since this book is designed for you, who is likely not a professional dog trainer. Second, keeping it simple and recognizable is important. The simpler the alert is the less chance of failure. Third, ask yourself, what is your dog capable of? What are you able to teach? What alert will fit our family?

Here a couple of examples of common alerts:

    ▪ <u>A Bringsel-</u> a stick that can hang on your dog's collar or hang on a hook in the house (see picture below). When your D.A.D smells low or high blood sugar he grabs the bringsel, sits, and holds it in his mouth. This is called a passive alert as you have to observe the dog to notice the alert. Bringsels were originally used in search and rescue work and are often used in agricultural and drug search dogs.

My therapy dog, Draco, demonstrating the use of a bringsel as a passive alert.

 ▢ The Bump- this alert is a little more physical while being silent. When your D.A.D. detects low or high blood sugar he simply bumps or paws the person. This is also a silent alert and less passive because there is physical contact.

 ▢ Bells- the D.A.D. uses a jingle bell that hangs or an electronic doorbell.

Common obedience-related alerts:
- o Paw on the lap- where your dog sits in front and puts a paw on your lap.
- o Dig- your dog digs an imaginary hole at your feet.
- o Running in circles- an alert where the dog runs in circles, as if chasing its own tail (this is Ping's alert to high blood sugar).

- And my personal choice:
- Bark- your D.A.D does a "Sit!" and barks for low and does a 'Down!' and bark for high (or vice versa).

How we decided Ping's alert

We knew Collin wouldn't be 10 years old forever. With Ping's life span, realistically and without any unforeseen complications, Collin should have Ping until he is about 20 years old. So we had to train Ping for a child, preteen, teenager, and even college student. We had to make sure the alert we chose would work for Collin now and fit his life as he grew. Kendra and I discussed places where it may be a problem if Ping barked or was intrusive. We debated this issue for days- weeks even. Then we added in the scenario of Collin as a freshman in college, asleep in his dorm room, and he drops low. We came to the conclusion that if Collin was ever in a situation where Ping barked an alert in public and someone got mad about it, then Collin didn't need to hang out there. Keep in mind that when a dog alerts there are signs that the dog will show before they alert. The D.A.D. begins to figure out the situation and has what I call a *tell*, which is unique body language that you will learn to read very easily before the alert. If the diabetic is engaged and aware of their surroundings, you can reward the D.A.D. before the bark-alert starts. However, if it is a situation where the diabetic is totally unaware and so low that they are in danger, then Ping would bark. We were also naturally lucky Ping doesn't bark at first, she always starts out with a couple of voiceless snaps of her jaw in the air before the full bark alert happens. This allows Collin to say "Let's check!" which is a Ping command for "Ping, please stop barking and wait patiently for your reward." If Collin were so low and unable to help himself, Ping would bark and run back and forth between Collin and anyone else in the room until rewarded. Would we want her nudging or sitting pretty with a bringsel? No- it wouldn't work for Collin.

Let's examine how you might think about choosing the right alert. First, train for the most dangerous scenario. Collin's danger time is at night and when he is alone. Collin doesn't always feel the low and can get a little spacey, thus he could easily ignore a passive alert. Second, what is your dog capable of learning? Not all dogs can learn everything. For example, I had an Australian shepherd, who was very intelligent and trained as a search and rescue dog. His searching skills were excellent and could find you in minutes, but he was afraid of loud noises, would not bark, and hated to hold anything in his mouth. If he was a D.A.D., we would have had an awful time teaching any of these alerts. However, most dogs can be taught to bark so usually it's an easy alert to teach. Lastly, what are you capable of teaching? This book is not for professional trainers. Instead, it is for laypeople that love dogs and want to train a D.A.D. themselves. Throughout this process, it's important to always keep it simple. Fewer steps are fewer chances of failure.

The last issue to think about is something that is very outside the box in terms of traditional dog training. The traditional view is to use one alert for high and another for low. But consider this scenario: Ping is alerting that Collin has low blood sugar. The next logical step is for Collin to test himself to see if his blood sugar is too high or low. Regardless of the D.A.D.'s alert, you always check your blood sugar levels. This means if Ping alerts to high sugar we test Collin the same way if she had alerted to low blood sugar- the outcome is the same. So for home-trained D.A.D.'s teaching one alert (to both high blood sugar and low blood sugar) will do the job because the result of the alert is always testing blood sugar levels. Remember, you always want to keep it simple.

In conclusion

Once you decide what the alerts will be, it is time to start teaching it to your dog. Think of the alert as a trick (for now). If your alert is to bark, give the command, "Bark!" or "Speak!", and the dog barks. Or say "Spin!" and your dog spins like a party trick. Do it often and for everyone you know. Keep it fun and always make the reward (either food or praise) worth it, so your dog is excited to do it over and over on command. Start this now so your dog has it down by the time you need to add the scent work.

Keep the alert simple without multiple steps. Stay away from complicated alerts, such as the dog runs and gets a bringsel from a hook and comes back and sits in front of the mother. There are too many things that can go wrong. What happens if you forgot to hang the bringsel on the hook? or it falls behind a piece of furniture as the dog pulls it off the hook? or someone closed the door to the room where the bringsel is? or what happens if the mom is in the bathroom with the door closed? When she opens the door, here sits the dog with the bringsel in his mouth sitting outside the door for the entire time but the mother never knew.

Ultimately, this is your decision and everyone's situation is different. Don't get hung up on what professional dogs do for an alert. Just because that's how they do it doesn't make it right for you and your dog. The most important thing is to find what works for you.

Chapter 8- Blood sugar meters

When we started training Ping in the spring of 2012, Collin was using a blood glucose (sugar) testing meter, and this book was written with that in mind. It worked well, but using a blood meter has its own challenges. When using a blood meter and a D.A.D. alerts, you have to test and make sure that the diabetic is low before the reward and praise is given. This is a problem under dog-training theory, as the reward should be given at the moment of the alert not a while after.

It can also be problematic because sometimes the D.A.D. will alert but the meter shows normal blood sugar levels. This may be a false alert (dogs make mistakes too) or because sometimes the D.A.D. can detect an impending low before the meter shows it. Ping has alerted 10 minutes before the blood glucose meter reflected a low. It is perfectly fine to train with a blood meter, but it does add a lot more complexity.

In February of 2013, Collin received a Continuous Glucose Meter or CGM. When using a CGM, a sensor is inserted under the skin on the stomach. This sensor measures the level of sugar in the tissue every 10 seconds and sends the information to a monitor that looks like a MP3 player. It records an average glucose value every 10 seconds and keeps that information for up to seven days. It will also tell you if the sugar is rising or falling. This makes a CGM an extremely valuable tool when training your D.A.D. because you can always see on the CGM if you're high, low, or crashing and can train appropriately.

Chapter 9- Collecting low blood sugar samples

Getting ready to train for low blood sugar

The first thing to decide is what low blood sugar number you want your D.A.D. to alert to. This is not a set number, because everyone's blood sugar numbers can be different. Consult your doctor on this decision. We wanted Ping to alert to below 80, but started training using samples of lower concentration. Go ahead and start collecting samples before you're ready to use them as it may take a little time to get enough samples from when the diabetic has low blood sugar levels (see below for instructions). Your goal is to collect a little stockpile of samples so you avoid running out of scent articles once you have started training. Try to collect samples of very low blood sugar levels because training starts with the lowest and juiciest samples as they are the easiest for the dog to smell.

Here is a generalized collection process:

1.   Have the diabetic spit (never use blood as a source of scent) on a square cotton or gauze cosmetic pad when they are low on blood sugar (the lower the better). Try not to handle the cotton square too much before or after if you're not the diabetic. If the diabetic sweats when they have low blood sugar, wipe off the sweat with a piece of cotton or gauze and store it with the saliva-sample. The diabetic can handle the cotton as much as they want to lay their scent.

2.   Place the cotton or gauze with spit on it (called a **scent sample)** in a ziplock bag or airtight bowl. Always mark the scent sample with the blood sugar number and date. You can turn the bag inside out and pick up the scent sample if you're handling it for the diabetic. Place the samples in the freezer and toss out the samples after 8 weeks.

Scent tubes and carriers

Further in the training process, after imprinting (covered in the next section), you will need to purchase some inexpensive equipment. You will need something to put the scent sample (gauze) in, called a scent tub, to have your dog find. I like to use something that a puppy can pick up in their mouth safely without the risk of swallowing. Whatever you choose to use needs to have holes or slits in it so the scent can flow freely. We used tubes from the diabetic test stripes with holes drilled into it or new fecal testing tubes from the vet. You can also use a cloth toy so you can play a little tug of war to celebrate your puppy's success. You will need several of these tubes and they should be identical. Once you use a tube, mark it so the tube is only used for low or high samples from then on. Containers can hold a scent for a long time; that means once you have used it to store low samples it will smell that way permanently. Do not put new low samples in old high bottles or vice versa.

Blood-test strip scent tubes. These tubes contain many holes that were made by pushing a hot nail through the plastic. The more holes the better!

Collin and Ping playing with a soft toy with scent sample inside.

Chapter 10- How scent travels

You cannot train a scent dog without understanding how scent travels. Search and rescue dogs follow what is called a scent cone. A scent cone is a cloud of dead skin cells that float through the air, which originates from the skin of each person and expands outward. Scientists are studying how dogs can smell when a person's blood sugar is low, and scientifically, it's still a mystery. It is safe to say that the scent (the smell of biochemical changes in the saliva and sweat) travels on air currents, and the scent cone theory can also be applied here to better understand how scent travels.

The smallest point of the cone starts at the person with diabetes and gets wider the farther away you get from the person. The dog picks up the scent of low blood sugar somewhere in the wider part of the cone and follows the scent to the narrowest end, which ends at the point of the cone, the person. The dog follows the scent by moving in and out of the scent cone. Simple enough, right? Wrong. Scent cones can be manipulated by other factors, such as wind when you are outside at a picnic, the heater in the car, air conditioned air indoors, or even something as simple as someone creating a current by opening a door in the house. Any change in air currents can distort and move the cone away from the dog. Understanding and being aware of air currents is essential. Always be thinking about how that scent is traveling to your D.A.D., and base the decision of where you position your D.A.D. in regard to air currents. If you are concerned about air currents in the home, you can do some simple experiments by using a poof of baby powder or smoke sticks used by the heating and air ventilation industry.

Chapter 11- How this is going to work

In the following chapters you will find detailed instructions for each step of the training process. First, I'd like to give you an overview of what is going to happen. My father often gave me advice to "KISS it! Keep it simple, stupid," and that truly applies to dog training. Everyone thinks training a D.A.D. is difficult, but it is much easier than you think... if you keep it simple.

Here are the five steps to training a D.A.D. outlined in this book. Let me repeat again that this is how we trained a diabetic alert dog. This is purely a starting point for your own training.

1. Imprinting - Link the scent of low blood sugar to a reward. This teaches your D.A.D. to identify the scent.

2. Bonding and playing - The D.A.D. must enjoy and always want to be with the diabetic. Encouraging games and activities will naturally build the bond between diabetic and dog while developing a healthy play drive.

3. Scent training - Continuing to teach the dog to identify and follow the scent cone.

4. Tell me! - Adding in the alert.

5. Link it to the child - The scent training is only done with the child.

6. Reinforce real time alerts- Practice and secure that the scent game is actually a job which happens all day and night.

Now that you see the game plan, read on to get a full understanding of how and why this works. To successfully train a D.A.D. you only need five simple steps. Don't let yourself get overwhelmed, and as my dad would say, K.I.S.S.!

Chapter 12- Feeding and imprinting

Feeding

D.A.D.s are on the job 24 /7 - without days off or vacations. Keeping your D.A.D. healthy and always on top of his game starts with the food you feed him. Today's dog food is a far cry from the dog food of yesteryear so do your research and pick a healthy food. Dog food companies are aware that the consumer wants a healthy choice. The one thing that is different about today's dog food is that ingredients are sometimes imported from other countries where they can become contaminated. So always check the bag as most companies will let you know if it's American made.

Follow the feeding instructions on the bag to insure you're feeding the proper amount. I supplement dog food with whole food such as lean meat, fruit, and vegetables when doing the scent drills. Find your dog's favorite food, maybe liver sausage, tuna, or apples, and use it to make your dog's successful completion of a scent drill extra special.

Imprinting

To begin imprinting, it is helpful to understand a quick science lesson. Pavlov was a scientist in the 1800's who did experiments on animal behavior. Pavlov's experiment started by giving hungry dogs food, while at the same time ringing a bell. As the experiment went on, the dogs would salivate and become excited with just the sound of the bell because they anticipated being fed. Pavlov determined that through imprinting the dogs would salivate at the sound of the bell due to an involuntary psychological association between the bell and their food.

This is a very important lesson that you will teach your D.A.D. We want your D.A.D. to salivate and get excited at the smell of low blood sugar, and we want it to be involuntary! The goal is if your D.A.D. is sleeping and smells low blood sugar, that they involuntarily start to salivate and wake up.

To accomplish this, start by dividing the food into four somewhat equal parts (you don't have to be exact). Pour one of the fourths into a paper bowl with at least 8-10 slashes or holes in the bottom. Utilizing throw-away paper utensils is by no means original, but has been used in different areas of dog training for a long time. It is especially useful with diabetic alert dog training as you can throw away the food bowl after each use to avoid contamination. If you're the diabetic always use your hand and handle the food, which will make the food smell like you. Then place a scent sample (the one with the lowest blood sugar levels you have on hand) in another bowl. You now have one bowl with the one fourth of the recommended feeding amount and one bowl with the scent sample. Place the bowl with the food on top of the bowl with the scent sample.

Your dog is going to eat with his nose down in the bowl while breathing in the scent of low blood sugar. Have the diabetic (always, if possible) hold the bowl at feeding time in a comfortable quiet place and calmly tell dog "good low, good low." Repeat with the other 3 parts of food. Try to drag it out and make it a pleasant experience every time.

Through this method, we are implementing Pavlov's theory. We are imprinting the smell of low blood sugar onto the pleasure of eating delicious food. The reaction you should eventually get is an excited and anxious work ethic. This happens because the D.A.D. associates the smell of low blood sugar with wonderful treats and games.

An example of the two bowl setup. The bowl on the left contains a piece of gauze that smells like the diabetic with low blood sugar. The bowl on the right contains dog food and has slits cut into the bottom. The bowl on the right can be placed in and on top of the bowl on the left, combining the scent of the low or high blood sugar with the reward of food.

Children and imprinting

Have your diabetic child hold the bowl every time the puppy eats. Use this opportunity to teach your child how to use their voice in a calm and comforting way while petting the puppy softly. This will reinforce the bond between the child and puppy and reduce the chances of your puppy developing guarding issues (some dogs feel the need to protect food, toys, and even real estate). This is a dangerous and unpredictable behavior.

Colin holding the two bowls, letting Ping eat, and telling her she is a good puppy.

The exercise links three very important things together: low scent + food + the diabetic, and teaches the puppy to seek out the scent and to move towards it to eat their food. This is what a D.A.D. does every time they smell low or high blood sugar; they catch the scent and follow the scent to the child. Doing this while imprinting reinforces that action. As the imprinting process progresses, feel free to make it fun and creative. Try playing a little bit of hide and seek with the puppy and child. The more fun the child has, the more fun the D.A.D. will have. And, happy and balanced dogs are the hardest working. Below is how your training might progress. This may takes days to weeks depending on how quickly the dog learns.

After a couple of days, move to a different spot but in the same room, to feed your puppy. Call your puppy or dog to come and eat by saying: "Where's your low?" While holding the bowl, allow your dog to eat and softly say "Good low!" Remember to maintain a happy tone during this stage of the training.

After a few more days, move out of the room to feed him and call the puppy to you by saying: "Where's your low?" in that same, happy voice. Continue to put the scent article between the bowls. Additionally you can increase the difficulty by sitting to feed your puppy in an adjacent room. Make sure to pick a spot in the next room that is visible through the doorway still. Don't worry if he is confused at first. If you need to call him a couple of times, go ahead. It is not a failure if you have to call multiple times; it is simply part of the learning process.

At this point, your dog is probably getting excited when he hears the food container open and the food being put in the bowl. Now, you need to get tricky and not let him hear or see the food. We want your dog to start using his nose. Again, after a few more days move to another spot and continue making this an enjoyable game.

Once your dog understands the game and is playing it successfully, stop calling him and instead say "Where's your low?" Make it difficult by filling the bowl, going to your chosen spot, and sit there, not calling him over. If he doesn't notice you can try shaking the food bowl a little bit to get their attention. As soon as your dog runs to you and puts their nose into the bowl (the magic moment the smell hits the nose) exclaim, "Good low!" in your happy training voice. Be patient before you give the hint by shaking the bowl. Your puppy is learning to work the problem and sometimes it takes a minute or two for them to realize what they are smelling.

Continue moving all over the house, always keeping the game positive. If your dog suddenly cannot find you and his scented dinner, go back to the last place and repeat it successfully. Then you can move on to the next spot. While you can maintain playing hide-and-go-seek with your puppy, this is a great game for a child to play with their D.A.D. Dogs always love the person that feeds them, helping with the bonding process. Puppies sometimes feel like they are higher in the pack than human children living in the home (especially dogs suited for this kind of work). So having a child holding the bowl while feeding puts the child higher in the pack than the puppy which will also reduce the possibility of food guarding. It's a fantastic way for your puppy and child to get to know each other.

The picture above shows Collin and Ping playing hide and go seek. Collin hides, out of sight, without letting Ping see where he is going. This game teaches: **1.** the dog to use their nose and not their eyes. **2.** reinforces that the D.A.D. has to pay attention to the scent cone regardless of being inside or outside the home **3.** helps develop problem solving ability in the dog. **4.** allows the handler to observe the D.A.D.'s body language. **5.** promotes bonding between the dog and child through an enjoyable activity!

Once your dog starts to get the game, move to places that your puppy can't see and be very quiet (see picture above). This is when your puppy will naturally use his nose, since he can't see or hear you, and he will be able to smell the low and the food. This should last about three weeks, but it can be longer if needed. You know you're ready to move on when he can always find you.

Reflections on imprinting

Imprinting is the foundation to your D.A.D.'s success. Here is a list of what your dog has just learned from this chapter alone.

1. What the scent of low blood sugar smells like.

2. How to find the low by following the scent cone. This is important because the diabetic will not always be sitting next to the dog. The D.A.D. will need to learn to move to the diabetic by following the scent cone and alert.

3. The two best things in a normal dog's day is dinner time and when his human plays with him. You are linking the low scent to that list. A D.A.D.'s best time of the day is when they smell the low and he gets to eat and play with his human.

This exercise is critical to your goal, and it teaches your puppy several things other than how to follow a scent cone and work through problems.

The "tell"

While you and your puppy are playing the feeding-searching game and when you start scent tube training drills, you will want to watch for what I call the "tell". The tell is the body language your dog exhibits the second the scent hits its nose. Training will be much easier if you learn to see the puppy's tell.

With Ping, when the scent would be exposed to the air she would stop whatever she was doing and freeze like a statue. Her ears would go up almost as if she thought she heard something, her nose would go up in the air, and then she would take off looking for where that smell was coming from. You will get used to watching for the "tell". It is so obvious it is almost as if you can see the scent hit their nose.

You must learn your puppy's tell because an important event is going to happen once your dog really understands that all the good things happen when he smells low blood sugar in the diabetic. You have to be able to look at your puppy and see the behavior (the tell) and realize the big moment is about to happen- the moment that your dog smells a real low and moves towards the child. Don't be fooled if the puppy starts smelling all over the room or along a wall. This is your puppy working the problem. Once he smells it, and as soon as he reaches the child, you need to have the biggest and grandest celebration ever. If you catch that magic moment, you will be well on your way to success!

Chapter 13- Play Games

Play play play... Find interesting games to play that stimulate the mind. Do not play tug of war, chase, wrestling, or all of those physical type games. While we may use that type of play later, you don't want to encourage rough play in a puppy. A puppy will not know when to turn off the rough play or when it's getting too rough and could hurt a child.

Developing a healthy play drive is integral. At this stage, play games that encourage your puppy to think and to look to you for fun. A couple of games for a young puppy are:

Game 1- Roll a tennis ball and allow your puppy to see the ball roll. When the puppy pounces on it mark the action with a command. You can say "Get it!" or "Fetch!" and call them back by saying "Come!" in a happy voice. As the game progresses, roll the ball in different directions, softly bounce it off walls, or roll it behind furniture. Make sure to keep it simple enough that your puppy can always get it.

Optional: You can also cut a hole in the ball and put a low scent sample inside.

Game 2- Get a wiffle or tennis ball and cut a hole large enough for food to easily fit through. Put a handful of their kibble in the hole and encourage your dog to roll the ball with their nose allowing the kibble to fall out of the ball rewarding the puppy.

Optional: You can also put a low scent sample inside along with the food to further reinforce the food-blood sugar connection.

Game 3- Get a muffin pan and a toy or ball for every cup. With you puppy watching, place a treat and a low scent sample in one cup and put a ball or toy in every cup (including the cup with the scent sample and treat so the toy covers it all). Encourage your dog to find it by saying, "Where's your low at"? Encourage your dog to pick up the toy or knock it out with their nose to get the treat. At first, let your puppy see you place the treat. As your puppy gets the idea, slowly make it more difficult by spinning the muffin pan so he doesn't know where it is visually or place it in the cup when the puppy can't see you do it.

Game 4- Fetch! Who doesn't love a good game of fetch or frisbee?

There are many games that can be enjoyed by you and your dog. Find games that work for you and remember to keep it fun!

Chapter 14- Time to start the scent work drills

So you made it this far; congratulations! Let's see if you're ready to move on to the next step. BONDING, ALERTING, IMPRINTING, and PLAYING are the four behaviors your D.A.D. should have down at this point. You now have a healthy puppy that loves you to the point that they want to be with you every minute and go every place you go. He loves to play and can play for at least 10 minutes without losing focus. You should also be able to move around the room, surrounding rooms, and even hide out of sight with the food dish and/or scent sample and your puppy should happily be able to figure out where you are (don't worry if it takes a minute or two). Your D.A.D. should be well on their way to being able to perform his alert on a verbal command and attending obedience class or working with a private trainer. Lastly, he or she should also be comfortable traveling and moving respectfully through the house.

Where's your low?

At this point, your puppy has learned that the low scent always means food and quality time with their favorite person. More importantly, he has started to learn to use his nose and not his eyes or ears. The next phase is a series of drills which will reinforce that your puppy can identify the low scent and follow the scent cone. It seems simple enough to us, but your puppy has to learn to follow the scent and figure out where it's coming from. You might think that your D.A.D. doesn't really need to learn the skill of following the scent because your D.A.D. will always be at your feet. However, in real life they aren't always right in your face.

Let me explain this further by sharing with you what happened between Ping and Collin one night. Collin was watching TV with his family and dropped low. Ping was sound asleep on the cool tile about 20 feet away and down a hallway, not able to see where Collin was sitting. Ping woke up, her nose went up in the air, she ran down the hall in the opposite direction only to do a quick U-turn directly to Collin and then alerted. Ping had caught the scent and woke up due to imprinting, followed the invisible scent cone, but turned the wrong way at the end of the hallway because the air current was carrying it in that direction. Because Ping knows how to follow a scent cone, she could smell that the scent was weaker going that direction so she made the decision to turn around and head toward the room Collin was in. This is why it's important to teach your puppy to work the problem and follow the scent cone.

Real time lows

Ping watching Colin test his blood sugar on a hiking trip.

When your child is testing their blood sugar levels, have your puppy sit and watch. When the meter shows a number that you consider low, say to your puppy, "Where's your low"? Afterward, call the puppy to the child and encourage the child to praise and reward the puppy with a real food treat. If the child isn't low, simply pat the dog on the head and tell him "Good sit." Repeat this <u>EVERY TIME, DAY OR NIGHT!</u>

Scent tube training guidelines

At this stage, we will begin to introduce your D.A.D. to the scent by using scent tubes. Before we get into the drills, here are simple rules to follow when doing this set of scenting drills.

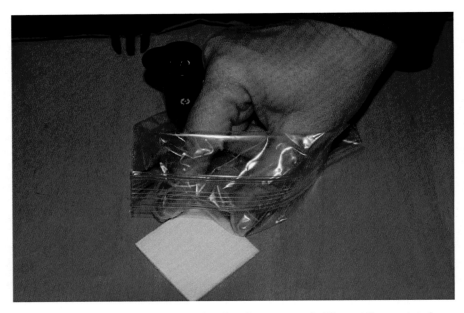

If you aren't the diabetic, be careful when handling the scent sample. We want the sample to be as pure as possible, and by touching it you run the risk of laying your scent on it.

- Always use your juiciest and lowest scent sample if possible. If the diabetic isn't handling it, be careful not to lay your own scent on it. A simple way to avoid this is to use the zip lock bag as your glove (as shown above).

- Use favorite treats. I like to use healthy whole food such as beef, chicken, liver, apples, carrots, or Ping's favorite, cheese. Only use real food for scent training to keep the reward special and be sure to find your puppy's absolute favorite.

- FUN FUN FUN! It has to be fun! Make it like a game. If you have had a bad day and don't feel like having fun, then I give you permission to skip it and do it tomorrow when you have the energy to have fun.

- Always mark when your dog hits on the scent tube, by saying, "Good low!" or "Yes!" and reward with a treat at the magic moment, which is the exact second the puppy finds the scent tube.

- Scent training should be done at least three times (or more if it is still fun) per day in short sessions never lasting longer than 10 minutes. Make sure to end on a positive note.

- Once your puppy figures out the game, include your child with diabetes in this game. This a fun game to play and your child can be involved. You can have them do all of it or a certain part depending on their age.

- Do not rush the process. This series of drills can take weeks. The time taken can depend on your consistency when training, how often you hit the magic moment, and of course, your dog's ability.

- Unless you are rewarding and praising at the magic moment, do not say a word. Although it is natural to want to talk, encourage, and praise him as they start to get close, what you are really doing is knocking them out of the zone by distracting them. Talking before the puppy solves the puzzle is the equivalent of you writing a letter in deep thought and all of a sudden a family member comes in and starts talking to you in a really fun tone. Not only do you lose your thought process but you most likely looked up and lost your visual place as well. We are (most of the time) able to go back right to the spot where we were distracted, but a puppy doesn't have that ability.

- Don't forget to keep your log as you will need it if you run into any hiccups.

- Learn your puppy's body language and get to know the tell (see chapter 12 for review), and be prepared to reward when your dog responds to a real-time low.

Drill #1 Low scent tube play game

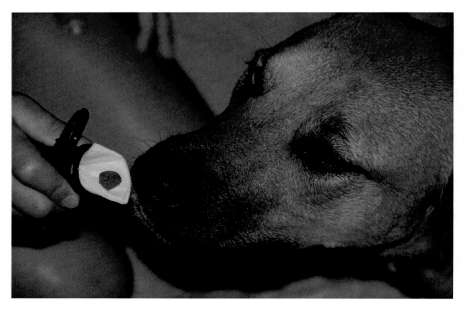

Ping smelling the scent sample and treat. After, the tube will be closed with the treat and the scent sample inside. This way the D.A.D. links the scent of low blood sugar with the treat.

Instructions:

1. Put a scent sample in a scent tube. Let your puppy smell and draw in the scent for as long as he likes. Then put a treat in the scent tube with the sample.
2. Get your puppy's attention and have him "Come!" to smell the scent tube.
3. When his tail starts to wag and ears perk up in excitement, say "where's your low!?" This gives your puppy the signal that the games are about to begin.
4. Give the tube a little toss or roll.
5. Once the puppy runs to it and the moment they smell it, say "Yes, good low!" Open the tube and let your puppy smell inside the tube and then pour the treat into your hand repeating "Good low!"

Ping demonstrating the proper distance between D.A.D. and scent tube in early training.

Repeat steps #1-5 in the same room to avoid making it exceptionally difficult. Always end with a success, and never let your puppy fail. You can avoid failure by giving your puppy a hint. A hint would be something like moving the dog closer to the scent tube or walking them past it. When you are doing scent training, it may seem like your puppy is taking too long to find the scent tube. You might wonder: how much time should you give them? Knowing when they are working the problem and when the puppy is wandering around distracted is an art. Give your dog a chance to work it through before you decide he can't do it.

Extra credit

Once your puppy can complete the game at least six times in a row, it is time to make the game harder while maintaining the same amount of fun. Below is a list of ideas you can incorporate (from easiest to hardest) to increase the challenge of the game. **Start with challenge A and work towards challenge R before moving onto drill #2.**

A. Roll the scent tube a short distance

B.   Roll it farther than before

C.   Roll it in different directions

D.   Give it a toss

E.   Toss it a little farther

F.   Toss it in different directions

G.   Set it in the middle of the floor

H.   Set it partially behind a table leg or something so the tube is partially hidden but be sure the puppy can still see it

I.   Near the same place, but place it totally behind the table leg

J.   Move it, while keeping it hidden to the puppy, to the next table leg in the same area

K.   Now no longer let your puppy see you hide it. Move him to another room or have your puppy do a sit & stay facing the other direction. Slowly hide it on the floor out of sight but always close to the last site.

L.   Hide it a little higher up like on top of a pot or box

M.   Move it around the room hidden on top a pot or box

N.   Hide at chair height

O.   Move it to different chairs

P.   Start alternating rewarding like you have been with the treat in the tube and then with the treat in your hand. Be sure to be ready because you want to have your hand extended to give him the treat as soon as you see the tell (the second the scent hits the nose).

Q.   Hide in different places around the room now while only giving them a treat with every 3 successful finds.

R.   Do it in other rooms in the house and only give the reward from your hand.

Eventually, you'll want to work up to harder challenges such as putting the scent tube farther away.

Now your puppy should understand the game and should be a master at finding the tube no matter how well you hide it. If he is still having a difficult time, rewind to where he started having problems (using your training log) and then start with the step before. If your puppy is finding the scent tube everywhere you hide it and is having fun doing it, focus on only rewarding with treats from the hand and not the scent tube. Success here means your puppy is really smelling and finding the scent tube because he identifies the low scent and not the treat. At first it was important to make him think that the two scents are linked because puppies love, love, love treats and we want him to find the low with that kind of enthusiasm every time.

Chapter 15- You found it. Now tell me!

Your puppy should be looking at you after he finds the scent tube for his reward. Now it's time to teach him to tell you that he found the low. Once again it's done in a series of drills. When you have completed drill #1 with all the possible variations (A-R), it's time to graduate to drill #2. Prepare everything exactly the same way. We want him to think we are going to play the same game.

Drill #2 Scent training with the verbal alert command

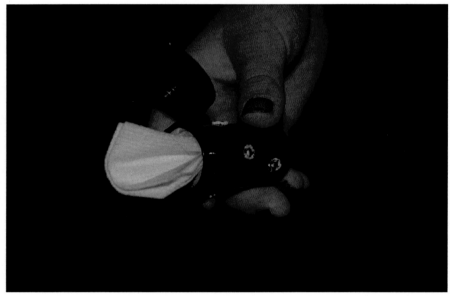

Drill #2 utilizes scent tubes without treats, as shown above.

1. Hide the scent tube (with a scent sample in it but no treat)
2. Let your puppy find it
3. When your puppy turns to you to get his reward, give your alert command that you have been practicing since Chapter 6. Your puppy will look at you like "hey, wait a minute I want my treat..."

But, as soon as he hears the verbal command of the alert he will think "Hey, I know that one." Then reward.

4. After a couple times he will understand that now the game is step one: find the low, step two: verbal alert, step three: reward.
5. Repeat this drill, moving the scent tube to all sorts of different places and distances, until your dog seems to do the alert as fast as you can give the command. After this move on to Drill #3, below.

Drill #3 Training without a verbal alert command

Kendra and Ping practicing without verbal commands

Once you get to the point that your puppy is alerting as fast as you can command him, the next thing you will do is drop the verbal command.

To practice scent training without verbal commands, your drill will look like this:

1. Hide the scent tube
2. When your puppy finds it, stare emotionless at your dog like you're waiting for something
3. When he alerts, then reward
4. Repeat until it becomes consistent

A note on false alerting: At some point your dog will alert when the child is neither high nor low. This will happen because either your dog is trying to figure out if the alert alone will get the same response, perhaps they are trying to trick you into treating, or maybe it was simply a mistake. Who knows which is actually true, but it is a relatively easy fix- just ignore it. Don't make eye contact with your puppy. Just go on with what you are doing and totally ignore your silly dog. However, a word of warning: be sure you are right! Dogs can be up to 20 minutes ahead of the meter, so you may be eating your words shortly if your child is low but the meter isn't showing it yet.

Chapter 16- Watching for the tell

A very important event is going to happen soon: your dog is going to catch a real low. It may not be with an alert, but he or she will smell it. You must be ready to reward it just like the drills.

If you're using a CGM meter, then you're going to know when your child is low or is crashing. You will be able to watch your puppy's behavior, and it will be easier to see the tell beforehand. Be prepared to reward at the magic moment when the scent hits the nose.

If you're blood testing, it doesn't allow you to deliver that reward at the magic moment (when the scent hits the nose) because you must be sure the blood sugar is low before you reward. You have to stop and test before rewarding the puppy. This is different than the drill where we reward the moment they show interest in the scent tube and you may possibly be in the process of learning the alert. You CANNOT reward until you're sure your child's blood sugar is really low. If you reward your dog when your child isn't really low, you're reinforcing your dog to alert when they really didn't smell the low. To accomplish this correctly is only a little tricky. When you see the tell, which is your puppy's body language that they smell a low keep your dog engaged by saying things like "Ok, I got it. Let's check!" in a very curious and happy voice. Have the puppy get into the habit of sitting and waiting for the confirmation (meter reading) of the low. Once you confirm the low then reward and celebrate.

Chapter 17- Alerting without the cue

We now have a puppy that knows what a low is and can find it anywhere and tell us by alerting. Now we need to drop the command "Where's your low?"

Drill #4 Find it without "where's your low"

1. Place your juiciest and lowest sample in your scent tube
2. Set the scent tube in an unexpected but obvious spot on the floor
3. Walk your dog by and when he stops to smell the scent tube (you may have to give your alert command just a couple of times so he understands it's the same game)
4. Mark the right behavior by saying "Yes! Good low!"
5. Reward and celebrate
6. Repeat until you can get several successes in a row
7. Continue to increase the challenge by hiding the scent tube and then move on to drill #5

Ping finding and pawing a scent tube that was hidden under the table.

Drill #5 Multiple scent tubes

1. Place your juiciest and lowest sample in your scent tube
2. Using another CLEAN AND NEVER USED scent tube, place both tubes on the floor about 2 - 3 feet away from each other
3. When your puppy goes to the correct tube, mark and reward
4. Continue adding more clean and unused tubes to the game and see if your puppy always goes to the correct tube

Chapter 18- Watch the pattern

At the beginning, I stressed consistency and always doing it the same every time. As your dog matures and becomes more accustomed to playing our little game, the consistency which served well can create a rut. Dogs are sometimes smarter than us and get cues from our patterns. This means if you always do it the same way, they may not be identifying the low from the smell but your pattern.

For example, while training Ping, since I didn't live with the family, Kendra would video tape the scent drills so I could see Ping's body language. It became obvious that every time Kendra picked up her phone to start videoing, Ping would start looking for her low. You could actually see her watch Kendra, then look around the room then look back at Kendra and the camera to confirm she was truly recording this. Then she would take off using her nose to find the low.

At first, we use the dog's ability to relate to patterns to our advantage but now it's time to challenge him. Be sure to change everything from the time of the day to the locations. Watch for things like the sound of the tube popping open when putting the scent into the tube the sound of the refrigerator door or cheese container opening. Your new goal is to be sneaky.

Chapter 19- Make it all about the numbers

At this point, your puppy should be able to find the scent tube hidden without the "Where's your low?" command and then alert when found, so now it's time to move up the numbers.

Drill #6 Move up to a high scent sample

Continue your scent tube drills, but now start using scent samples that are closer to normal blood sugar levels. If you were working scent samples at the 50 mark, move up to 54 and then to 56, and so on, up to the number that you want them to alert at. Pick a sugar level that's low enough to worry you but high enough that you can correct the situation in time. With Collin, we wanted Ping to alert to anything below 70.

So you worked your lowest scent samples and now are moving up to higher ones. Repeat this drill until your puppy proves that he can hit on all the scent samples below the number you set as their highest low number.

Chapter 20- Lose the tube

It's time to lose the scent tube. Now, when doing your drills, put the scent samples in different carriers. Use your imagination. It can simply lay on top of something or in a zip lock bag in bowls, cups, or even ashtrays. This drill drives home the fact that the low can be anywhere at any time and it doesn't look like a scent tube when found.

Drill #7 Scent training with no tube

1. Start out by using a low number sample and move up to higher ones as success and finding them dictates (going back to a low sample isn't a step backward, it is creating a smoother transition to no tube)
2. Place scent sample in a cup, bag, or on a plate
3. Bring the puppy into the room
4. Watch for the tell
5. Alert and reward

Chapter 21- Bring it home

From this chapter onward, no more hide and go seek games. It's time to link the activity to your child. From now on, the only place the low can be found is your child.

Drill #8 Scent sample and child

1. With a scent sample, have your child sit on the floor and place the scent sample sitting on the floor right next to them.

2. Have the child hold a treat in their hand

3. Bring the dog into the room. He will naturally run to the child sitting on the floor (no dog will resist that). When the puppy gets there, he will smell the low. Have your child to say "Yes, good low!" and reward. If the child is too young, you can mark and reward or both of you can do it together.

4. Repeat until the dog and child get the game and can do it successfully many times in a row.

Extra credit

As the child and dog successfully complete the game, increase the difficulty by introducing these challenges:

    A.   Move the child into a chair and repeat the drill

    B.   Move the scent sample higher. You can put it in shirt pocket or in a hat. Repeat until it becomes easy.

    C.   Have the child walk around the room and open the zip lock bag while having the dog follow it while moving.

    D.   Try it in the car, the bathroom, the deck... everywhere you can think of!

Drill #9 Introduce testing

In a real world situation, we wouldn't reward the D.A.D. until the testing meter confirms a real low. Your D.A.D. needs to learn to wait for the reward. At first, it was important to reward at the magic moment that the scent hit the nose and we saw the tell. In the previous drills our scent sample was taken when we knew Collin was low. But in the real world, Ping would alert and then we would test to see if Collin was low. In this drill we are teaching the dog to wait till after testing to confirm the low and then receive the reward. Without knowing for sure that the child is low we might end up with a dog that would just alert and expect a reward. Don't be crushed if your dog tries to get a treat without a real low. It will happen. It's time to add another link to our training chain... "Let's check!" our blood sugar.

Ping tell-ing when Collin gets home from school. Note the ears are up as Ping approaches Collin.

For this drill, try to recreate the atmosphere when lows occur. For example, have your family watch TV and have the diabetic child pop open the low scent tube. Your D.A.D.'s nose should go up in the air and run over to the child and alert. Instead of rewarding say, in a happy and curious voice, "Let's check!" and grab the meter and then "Let's check." To do this, tell your D.A.D. to "Sit!" next to the child or on the floor next to the child. Repeat the words and make eye contact to keep the dog engaged.

Test the child and even if they aren't low, and for training purposes pretend they are. So reward the dog and praise them in a celebratory voice. Training tip: the best time to do this drill is during times when the child would be testing anyway. Repeat this drill a couple of times per day for as many days as it takes. You will know it's time to move on when the D.A.D. alerts and sits in its place to wait.

Extra credit

A.   Repeat the drill in new places
       a.   Baseball games
       b.   In the car
       c.   At a relative's house
B.   Change the time of the drill
       a.   Repeat the drill in the morning
       b.   Try the drill at night

Notice Ping's body language. She looks determined, makes strong eye contact and her ears go back which is the "tell", followed by the barking alert.

Collin tests his blood sugar.

Chapter 22- Nighttime

This is often the most important time for your dog to be on top of his game because it can be the most dangerous time for a child to drop low. However, it is also the time when your D.A.D. is sleeping and could miss an alert to a low. There are several common reasons for failure at night:

1. **The D.A.D. is in deep sleep**. Just like humans, dogs have different stages of sleep. If a D.A.D. had a long, tiring day or maybe didn't get their usual naps he may be just sleeping too deeply. The age of a dog can play a part as well. Younger and older dogs seem to sleep sounder. And, of course, an unhealthy dog may sleep deeper.
2. **The dog fell asleep too far away** and the scent is moving away from them.
3. The child may have rolled over and covered their head with a pillow or buried their face in the blankets.
4. **An air conditioner or heater kicked on,** changing the movement of air away from your D.A.D.
5. Plus many more...

nighttime alerts.

There are some things that we just can't control and, like humans, dogs are not perfect. They are NOT computers that we can turn on and program. You have to realize there is an error factor. But, we can try to eliminate as many of the errors as possible by good, solid training. You also need to think about the situation and have an understanding of issues that affect

Let's go through each common problem and find a possible solution or at least reduce its frequency:

1. Sleeping too deeply
   a. Be aware if your dog is being run ragged. Give your D.A.D. the opportunity to rest on days that can be overly tiring.
   b. If your dog is young, he isn't ready to be on duty 24/7. Likewise, if they are too old and are sleeping through lows please start consulting with your vet to see if there is a medical reason. Sometimes taking off some weight, changing foods, or increasing exercise and play can make a big difference.
   c. If an older dog is continuously failing, you may consider retirement and starting a new puppy. If you choose to start training a new puppy for your second D.A.D., don't be surprised if the elder D.A.D. perks up and starts working again; it's just the way it works.

2. Dog sleeping too far away
   a. Every time- and I mean every time- you walk in that room and the D.A.D. has moved to the floor or the end of the bed call them back up to the closest spot to the child's mouth and praise them.
   b. You can also teach your dog the "Place!" command. This can be done several different ways and is often a command taught in obedience programs. "Place!" can be a place such as the child's bed or it can be a rug or piece of fabric that can be moved to different locations.
   c. For example, when I was training my search and rescue dogs I used a small piece of rug, like a carpet sample, and called it *place*. I trained my dogs to go sit on that rug every time I said "Place!" and to not leave that *place* unless I called "Come!" or "Return!" It didn't matter where the carpet was- it could be on the floor in the back of my SUV or in the middle of a field with other dogs sitting next to it. No matter where that rug was when I said "Place!" the dog went there and sat.

3. Child covering their face
   a. If this is a problem, sew the pillows to the mattress pad or sheets so they can't be pulled over their face. If it's the blankets, make sure they are tucked into the foot end so the child can't pull them up. You can also use lighter weight blankets. Depending on

your dog, this may not be a problem, but be aware that it could. Keep a log of missed alerts and how your child was sleeping.

4. Air conditioning or heat kicks on and changes air current
    a. Use smoke sticks, which are often used by ventilation experts, to see how the AC or heat effects the air current in your child's room. You will be able to see how the air moves through the room and figure out if there are areas that the scent may be sucked away from. Once you know this you can discourage your D.A.D. from making himself comfortable there.

Having addressed the most common nighttime issues, let's get started on conditioning your D.A.D. for nighttime work.

Nighttime Conditioning Drill #1

1. Use the lowest scent sample you have and place it in a scent tube (for easy handling) and place the scent tube in a ziplock bag or airtight container.
2. Have your dog's favorite food ready for a reward.
3. At night, when your dog is sound asleep with the child, sneak into the room like a ninja and pop open your container.
4. When the dog's eyes open, reward and mark it with "Good low!"
5. Don't be concerned with if the dog hears you or if you think they smell the treat because what we are teaching them is to wake up. If they smell the treat, then remember that the treat is a link to the smell of the low… we want them to always smell the low with the image of the reward. If they hear you and wake up, it's ok to still follow through with the drill. You go in and out of the room all the time at night to check blood sugar, so they have to get used to it. And if some of the times they get a reward and a pat on the head, they will be more anxious to tell you to come.
6. Once your dog awakens easily by the scent, move on to the next drill.

Nighttime Conditioning Drill #2

This drill is simply teaching the dog that the same rules apply as the alerts given during the day. Your dog needs to understand that this is the chain of events: I smell my low. I alert my people that the child is low. We test and make sure they are low. I am right. I have done my job. I get my reward!

1. Use the lowest scent sample you have and place it in a scent tube (for easy handling) and place the scent tube in a sealable plastic bag or airtight container.
2. When you go into the child's room to test, pop the scent sample under the dogs nose and when he wakes up say "Good low! Let's check!"
3. Proceed with checking and no matter what the number actually is pretend it is low.
4. Give your dog the verbal alert (example: "Speak!") and reward.

Extra Credit

If your child sleeps in your bed, a bed of a sibling from time to time, naps on the couch, or sleeps over at Grandma's, then practice this drill there so the dog understands that it's always game on even though they aren't in the child's bedroom.

Chapter 23- Are you high?

Once your puppy is accomplished at finding lows, which means not only successfully completing all the drills with ease but catching real time lows, you can move on to highs. This will be significantly easier since the D.A.D. has already learned the rules to the game and loves to play. To start, you will need to collect high samples and get a stockpile going just like you did with low samples. You will need brand new scent tubes and an airtight container to keep the samples in. **DO NOT RE-USE ANYTHING FROM THE LOW BLOOD SUGAR TRAINING DRILLS.** You do not want anything that could remotely smell like the low samples to be near items that should smell like high samples. If you choose to ignore this warning, you could confuse your D.A.D. As with lows, handle all samples carefully. Do not lay your scent on the sample if you're not the diabetic. Use the drills below to train your dog to alert to high blood sugar levels. Follow the same tips and guidelines as before, and only move onto the next drill when your dog can flawlessly perform the drill multiple times in a row.

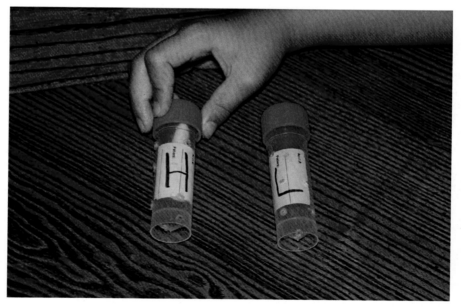

Example of separate high and low tubes used during Ping's training. Training tip: make low and high tubes identical so the D.A.D. is forced to use his nose and not their eyes.

High Drill #1- Where's your high?

1. Place the highest scent sample you have in your arsenal into the scent tube.
2. Let your dog smell the sample for as long as he or she wants.
3. Roll or toss the scent tube a short distance (or use whatever method you found worked when training low). As you toss it, say "Where's your high?!"
4. When your D.A.D. runs to the tube, tell him "Good high!" and reward on retrieval.
5. Repeat, tossing the scent tube in all directions. Mark the action with "Find your high!" and reward and praise with "Good high!" Be sure to make it a fun game and use his favorite treats.

High Drill #2- Can you find it?

1. Place the highest scent sample you have into the scent tube.
2. Place the tube behind a table leg or something that hides the scent tube but will allow it to be found easily. Keep it simple by hiding it close to where you are standing.
3. Mark it with "Where's your high?" If your D.A.D. doesn't go right to it, with the enthusiasm you've seen with low, don't panic! Give your D.A.D. a moment to figure it out. While he is thinking, do not say anything to him. We often feel like he didn't hear us or maybe they need to hear the command again. All that does is interrupt the process.
4. If your D.A.D. doesn't find it, then walk over and point it out using an excited voice, like you were surprised to find that high hiding there. Repeat hiding until he gets the new game.
5. Reward when the D.A.D. finds the sample and happily say "Good high!"

High Drill #3- Hide and Seek High

1. Place the highest scent sample you have into the scent tube.
2. Hide the tube without the D.A.D. watching. Making it more difficult each time as long as they are easily finding the tubes. If there are problems, it is okay to let him watch while you place it. Just remember to keep it positive and have fun. Don't move on to more difficult problems until your D.A.D. has mastered the level before. If the problem continues and your D.A.D. doesn't catch on, go back to Drill #1.

3. Be sure to continue to use the verbiage: "Find your high!" and "Good high!"
4. Reward when the high is found.

High Drill #4- Tell me

1. It is time to chain the alert as we did before.
2. Place the highest scent sample you have into the scent tube.
3. Hide it in a semi difficult place.
4. Ask your D.A.D. "Where's you high?"
5. When your dog arrives at the scent tube, with excitement in your voice, give your verbal command for the high alert. For example, with Ping, we used "Spin!" instead of our normal low alert.
6. When your D.A.D. gives the alert, reward your dog!
7. Repeat until he or she alerts before you can say the command.

Drill #5- Link it to the child

1. Place the highest scent sample you have in your arsenal into the scent tube.
2. Have the child carry the scent tube and hide it in different places making it fun for both of them.
3. Tell your D.A.D., "Where's your high?"
4. Once your D.A.D. sniffs the high, he should alert.
5. Reward after the alert.

Drill #6- The numbers game

For this drill, work your way down to the lower numbered scent samples. Be sure to stay in the high range and never drop below the range you and your doctor have determined as 'high' for the diabetic. Continue to play the hide and go seek game, but encourage the D.A.D. to find the high without the verbal command. You can use little tricks such as having the child walk by with the scent sample or you can sit down by the diabetic and call the dog to you. Remember that you need to be ready for the moment that the D.A.D. picks up on the scent without the verbal command. As soon as you see the tell give the command for the high alert. Only give the command for the alert a couple of times just so they know that is what you want. After a couple of successful times, wait for them to tell you with the alert and then reward.

Extra Credit

Place a low scent sample in a low scent tube and a high scent sample in a high scent tube, then label each with a marker. Then, grab three new scent tubes for this set of extra credit.

1. Extra credit #1
    a. Place the three brand new tubes on the floor along with the low scent tube.
    b. Tell your D.A.D. to find his low.
    c. Wait for the alert when he finds it.
    d. Reward.

2. Extra credit #2
    a. Place the brand new tubes on the floor along with the high scent tube.
    b. Tell your D.A.D. to find his high.
    c. Wait for the alert when he finds it.
    d. Reward.

3. Extra credit #3
    a. Place the three brand new tubes on the floor along with the low and high scent tube.
    b. Tell your D.A.D. to find his low.
    c. Wait for the alert when he finds the low tube.
    d. Reward.
4. Extra credit #4
    a. Continue changing back and forth from finding the high to finding the low. Remember to keep it a fun game

If your dog can't figure out which one is which, be sure to help them. These drills are about teaching not testing. If your dog can't find the tube, go over by it and point it out. Ask for the proper alert and reward. If your dog picks up the wrong one, point out the right one and ask for the proper alert and reward.

Chapter 24- Let the fun continue!

Depending on the age of the child with diabetes, an additional fun activity to do with your D.A.D. is canine agility. Agility is a dog sport where dogs are taught to run through obstacle courses, which can involve leaping over dog jumps, doggy teeter-totters, going through tunnels, and weaving between poles (and more), all on command. In the dog training world, this sport is always done in a fun and high energy atmosphere with little or no negativity. This is a great reward because most dogs end up loving agility. But, there's more to it than just a great reward and energy outlet for your dog. Here are just a few reasons why I recommend agility:

- Your D.A.D. will be able to blow off nervous energy.
- Your D.A.D. will learn to listen for commands and sharpen his reaction time.
- Your D.A.D. will build confidence in moving around on shaky surfaces such as dog walks and teeter-totters.
- Agility is done off leash. This forces the handler, you, to learn to control the dog without a leash.
- It is a great sport for a child to be involved in as a junior handler.
- If your diabetic child does it, he or she can learn when and how to deliver a command.
- Agility will keep both handler and dog healthy because it's a great source of moderate exercise.
- Agility helps build a bond between the dog and handler.
- The best part is both handler and dog have fun doing this, so it doesn't even seem like training.

Once you have successfully completed obedience training, ask your instructor for a recommendation on agility programs in the area that would be suitable for a child. Call and speak to the agility instructor and explain your situation. The dog training community supports junior handlers (after all most of us were one at one time) and often have special programs dedicated to kids. The most important factor is that everyone should have fun and enjoy the beautiful relationship you develop when doing agility.

Chapter 25- What could possibly go wrong?

Because there are so many factors in training a dog it would be impossible to address each and every problem in a book (without turning it into an encyclopedia). But there are a couple of tricks a trainer can use to solve problems.

- When teaching a dog a new command, always break it down to small steps. If the dog isn't able to figure out what you are asking him to do, then break it down to even smaller steps until he can understand.

- When a dog successfully completes one of the smaller steps, reinforce it by repeating it successfully at least seven times in a row. Then, you and your dog can move on to the next step.

- Sometimes training may be moving along and all of a sudden you hit a brick wall and your dog can't learn the next step. The most important tip is to not allow neither you nor your dog to get frustrated. Simply back up to the last step and repeat it several times successfully and then move on.

Chapter 26- Today

Today, Collin is a healthy and happy teenager who is proud of the wonderful service dog that he helped train. For Ping, the training will never stop. Collin is planning to continue training her in agility for fun. Ping will always need to be challenged to keep her nose sharp, through regular drills and tricky scent problems with huge rewards. The games will continue to keep Ping engaged no matter how experienced she becomes.

I sincerely hope the information in this book gives you some insight as to what it takes to train a diabetic alert dog at home. I hope someday there will be training classes in every town for D.A.D.s. In the meantime, I will pray for a cure and hope in the future that every child with type 1 diabetes has a dog to cuddle with at night.

The Ping Project Today

For more information on the Ping Project and diabetic alert dogs, visit www.thepingproject.com You can also find updates on the book, related canine content, and more. Our site is a great resource for questions and continuing projects, but also the best way to contact Shari about D.A.D.s and dog training. Please use the website if you have any questions or concerns and visit often for new content!

Glossary

Alert: A change in a dog's behavior, such as a bark, bump, or ringing of a bell that alerts you to low or high blood sugar.

Bond: The relationship between dog and person.

Capturing: A term used by dog trainers to describe a training technique. A trainer captures a natural dog behavior by marking it with a command and reward in order to get the dog to repeat it on command.

Count: Refers to the reading on the glucose meter when a sample is taken or when a dog alerts.

False alert: When your dog alerts and the child is not actually low or high.

Guarding: A dog behavior when the dog acts aggressively because they feel something they own is going to be taken away. Guarding most commonly occurs while eating (guarding food) but guarding can also include an area such as your lap, its bed, or yard.

High: Refers to elevated sugar level.

Low: Refers to low sugar level.

Mark: Marking a dog behavior is matching a command to the behavior. For example when you pat the bed signaling for your dog to jump up. If you add the command "up" every time, eventually you will be able to say "up" and get the same results.

Magic moment: Is the exact moment the dog has completed a command.

Number: See *count*, above.

Olfactory cells: The receptors in a dog's nose that catch scent. Dogs have many more times as many of these cells as humans, which allows them to smell things we cannot.

Reward: The pay-off for a job well done. Rewards can be food, play, or praise.

Scent sample (sometimes called scent article): The piece of gauze with saliva and sweat from the diabetic used to train the dog.

Scent tube: The container that houses the scent sample when training. Scent tubes can be literal tubes or anything else you can think of to hold the scent tube.

Tell: The body language a dog displays at the moment they catch the scent. Most of the time it is obvious, but it can be as subtle as a change in tail or ear position.

Test to correct: This phrase means that even experienced D.A.D.s are not 100% accurate. You always need to test blood sugar levels after an alert. Never try to correct blood sugar levels using the dog alone. Correct it by using appropriate meters or other tests.

Training log: The record of your training sessions.

Acknowledgements

Writing this book would be impossible without the support and help of family and friends. A big, special thank you to the Chesney family for letting me document their time training Ping. Thank you to my son, Jonathan Finger, for editing and the late night debates. I couldn't have done it without you.

I'd also like to thank all my friends/editors that not only helped me by checking my grammar but also encouraged me to do something outside of my comfort zone. After all, I am a dog trainer, not an English major. A special thank you to my dearest friend Phyllis Campagna, who is not a dog person but took the time to read and edit it so we would be sure that even someone without dog knowledge could use this book. I'd also like to thank Kay Boyer, Walter Hahn, Bob Finger, and Daniel Finger for their help along with June Fischer-Lang who reviewed this book several times to make sure it was easy to follow and did a final edit. Thank you to Anna Ellsworth for letting Collin and I do agility at her training facility for free; thank you so much for helping someone that you didn't even know. I'd also like to thank Mary Mazzeri, who inspired me at the age of 13 during a park district dog obedience class and continues to be my go-to trainer when I can't figure out a behavior problem. Lastly, thanks to Steve Costello for his help with the legal advice regarding the book.

Made in the USA
Middletown, DE
08 December 2017